IN HIS LIKENESS

GOD'S HOLINESS AT WORK IN US

IN HIS LIKENESS

GOD'S HOLINESS AT WORK IN US

EVERETT LEADINGHAM, editor

Though this book is designed for group study,
it is also intended for personal enjoyment and
spiritual growth. A leader's guide is available
from your local bookstore or your publisher.

BEACON HILL PRESS
OF KANSAS CITY

Editor
Everett Leadingham
Assistant Editor
Jeremy Coleson
Director of Curriculum
Merritt J. Nielson

Copyright 2007
Beacon Hill Press of Kansas City
Kansas City, Missouri

ISBN: 978-0-8341-2274-1
Printed in the United States of America

Cover Design
Chad A Cherry
Interior Design
Sharon Page

10 9 8 7 6 5 4 3 2 1

CONTENTS

SALVATION— WHAT IS THAT?

BY RANDY HODGES

The story goes that Lois was married to Emmitt, a master penny-pincher. Emmitt was also a bit eccentric. Though he was paid well, he and Lois lived frugally, largely due to Emmitt's insistence that 20 percent of every check be saved—by stuffing it under their mattress. (Emmitt did not trust banks.) Emmitt often reminded Lois that the money would come in handy in later years.

At age 60, Emmitt was struck with cancer. Near the end, he made Lois promise, in the presence of his brothers, that she would put the money he had stashed away in his coffin so he could buy his way into heaven.

Everyone knew Emmitt was a bit odd, but this request was sheer craziness. Yet, Lois promised, assuring both Emmitt and his brothers that she would do as he asked.

Emmitt soon died, and Lois was a woman of her word. The morning following Emmitt's death, she took the entire sum of nearly $26,000 to the bank, where she deposited it. Lois then wrote a check for the full amount, which she promptly placed in the casket.

Emmitt's odd plan of trying to buy his way into heaven shows his ignorance of what God's Word tells us about how we really can come to live with God in heaven forever. The Word presents a plan of salvation that is marvelous and wonderful. Let's consider the matter of salvation by finding God's answer to this simple question:

WHAT DOES IT MEAN TO BE SAVED?

God's Word wonderfully explains the experience of salvation in ways we can better understand. Often, God relates heavenly things (like salvation) to things we already know and grasp in life. Yet, no one image fully explains all the wonders of salvation. So, Scripture uses a variety of images to help us better understand what it means to be saved.

Imagine a beautiful, flawless, intricately cut diamond. From one angle, the light marvelously sparkles with fiery splendor. Turn the gem just a bit and the view changes, revealing yet another marvelous image. The possibilities seem endless. Yet, with all the possible views, it remains the same diamond. Like the beautifully cut diamond just described, Scripture presents salvation by employing a variety of "views" to reveal more of the whole of salvation to us. Each view touches on another marvelous aspect of the great gift that God offers each of us. The "scriptural images" which follow help us to better grasp some of the wonder of what it means to be saved by God.

To be saved is to be delivered from bondage.

Apart from God, sin enslaves us, leaving us helpless to free ourselves. Though we want to break free and do that which is good and right, sin has us in its powerful grasp; and, in our own strength, we are unable to break free.

However, *God excels in the business of deliverance.* He delivered His people, the Israelites, from bondage to the Egyptian pharaoh. Over and over, God delivered David from danger and enemies. Just before this runt of a young boy stepped on the battlefield to engage the giant warrior Goliath, David remembered all the times God had delivered him. He expressed his confidence in God: "Your servant has killed both the lion and the bear; this uncircumcised Philistine will be like one of them, because he has defied the armies of the living God. The LORD who delivered me from the paw of the lion and the paw of the bear will deliver me from the hand of this Philistine" (1 Samuel 17:36-37).

And God delivered David.

God delivered Daniel from the den of lions. He delivered Jonah from the belly of the great fish. He delivered the apostle Paul from the hands of violent attackers, from the raging sea, from the plans of evil men, and from many other dangers. *God excels in the business of deliverance.*

God can deliver you too. He wants to deliver you from sin's bondage. If you are enslaved by sin, God wants to set you free. If you are enslaved by alcohol and unable to help yourself stop drinking, God wants to set you free. If you are addicted to nicotine and the "tobacco monkey" won't get off your back, God can set you free. If you are caught up in Internet pornography, God can set you free. Your inability to control your gambling problem may continue to grow until it destroys you and perhaps your family too. But God can rescue you and set you free. If you are held captive to illicit drugs, you can continue in the control of drugs until they rob your life of all that is good, or you can turn to God who wants to set you free. *God excels in the business of deliverance.*

Being enslaved by any sin that controls, dominates, and tyrannizes us is not salvation. It is slavery. And God's Word makes it clear that every one of us has sinned. Without God's intervention, we all are held captive by sin. Our sin may or may not be obvious to those around us.

Nevertheless, Jesus Christ came to set us free! And He will set us free, if only we will ask. "The LORD is my rock, my fortress and my deliverer . . . in whom I take refuge" (Psalm 18:2). God wants to release us from sin's power over us so that we can be freed to give ourselves to God. To be saved is to be delivered from sin's life-destroying bondage. *God excels in the business of deliverance.*

To be saved is to be treated by God as if we had never sinned.

The picture that Scripture paints of the moral condition that all humans possess apart from Christ is not pretty. The picture of our moral condition is painted in dark colors, which reveal that we are sinners separated from God and His holiness. The picture grows even darker as we see ourselves as having no righteousness in us. Because we are so far separated from God, unless something drastic changes us, our final destiny will be outer darkness and eternal separation from God. Apart from God's intervention, we are all headed for judgment and eternal destruction.

But God stepped in to do something in Christ Jesus about our sinfulness. He takes the dark picture that depicts our moral nature and "repaints" it in lighter and brighter colors. That is just what God does for us in justifying us.

To help us understand salvation better, the Bible grabs the word "justification." It means that God does not respond to us as the guilty, condemnation-deserving persons we are. Rather, when we take Jesus as our personal Savior, God forgives us and begins treating us as if we had never done anything wrong. God justifies us. Justification means God treats us "just-as-if-I'd never sinned." He provides us with a righteousness that is not earned, but so very needed.

"This righteousness from God comes through faith in Jesus Christ to all who believe. There is no difference, for all have sinned and fall short of the glory of God, and are justified freely by his grace through the redemption that came by Christ Jesus" (Romans 3:22-24). And the great news is that this change in the way God treats us is available to everyone who will turn from their sin and, by faith, take Jesus Christ as their Savior. In justifying those who turn to Jesus, God transforms the way we relate to Him. Where we were His enemies separated from God by our sin, once we are justified, we become God's friends. The change in our relationship with the Heavenly Father is huge. Before, we were alienated, separated, and estranged enemies; but now, we become forgiven, accepted friends. It's a total turnaround. It's a new relationship with God.

God offers us pardon and forgiveness that we do not deserve, and He provides acceptance that we could never earn. This amazing gift of a totally changed relationship with God is summed up in the word "justification."

To be saved is to be treated by God as if we had never sinned.

To be saved is to be adopted into God's family.

In the youth group of a church I once served, there was a teenage girl who was tall, thin, blond, and athletic. Kim was a competitive swimmer, using her God-given body and strength to excel at a sport she loved. When you looked at Kim's parents, it was not hard to see where she got her long, athletic build. Like Kim, both her mom and dad were tall and trim.

One day soon after meeting Kim, I commented to her parents how obvious it was that Kim was their child. Their response knocked my socks off: "She's adopted!" I could hardly believe it. She looked an exact younger image of her parents, yet they assured me it was true—Kim was not their child by birth, only by adoption. She not only looked like her parents, but she obviously loved and was loved by them. No doubt about the family relationship—Kim really was their child.

The relationship of Kim to her parents beautifully depicts what happens to us when we are saved. Scripture says it like this: "For you did not receive a spirit that makes you a slave again to fear, but you received the Spirit of sonship [or adoption]. And by him we cry, 'Abba, Father.' The Spirit himself testifies with our spirit that we are God's children" (Romans 8:15-16).

When God saves us, He invites us into His family. He

sets us free to enjoy the full benefits of belonging to His very own family. This wonderful reality becomes ours as we give our hearts to Jesus. In the Book of Galatians, Paul expresses this very truth, saying, "You are all sons of God through faith in Christ Jesus" (3:26).

To be saved is to be adopted into God's family.

To be saved is to be born again.

"Jesus declared, 'I tell you the truth, no one can see the kingdom of God unless he is born again'" (John 3:3). To be born again is to have the Holy Spirit make us over again, to make us new from within. It is to have God re-create us from the inside out.

To be saved is to be born again.

There are many other images that Scripture uses to tell us about salvation.

To be saved is to be reconciled to God.

Apart from Jesus Christ and His salvation, we're at war with God. We are His enemies. Instead of fighting alongside God in His war against evil, we position ourselves as rebels who are asserting ourselves and our will to have our own way.

However, when we are saved, we surrender ourselves to the supremacy of God. We quit opposing Him and surrender ourselves to Him. In doing so, we say, "I no longer wish to fight against You. Instead, I wish to join with You."

By God's grace, He allows us to give up being His enemy in order to become His friend. This is what Paul says in his letter to the church at Corinth: "God was reconciling the world to himself in Christ, not counting men's sins against them" (2 Corinthians 5:19).

To be saved is to become God's friend by reconciling with God.

To be saved is to be brought from darkness into light.

"He has rescued us from the dominion of darkness and brought us into the kingdom of the Son he loves" (Colossians 1:13).

To be saved is to be brought from darkness into light.

To be saved is to have the opportunity to start over again.

"If anyone is in Christ, he is a new creation; the old has gone, the new has come!" (2 Corinthians 5:17). In salvation, God gives us a second chance. A golfer would call it a "mulligan." A child may call it a "do-over." In life, the chance to start over again is called a "miracle."

To be saved is to have the chance to start over again.

To be saved is to begin the journey of holy living.

It is sanctification begun. Theologians refer to it as "initial sanctification." They mean that when we are saved, God plants within us a holy desire to move closer and closer to Him, to become more and more like Him. He offers us the chance to begin growing, developing, and maturing. He molds and shapes us, increasing our likeness to His glorious Son, Jesus Christ. The longer we serve Him, the longer we walk with Him, the more we become like Him.

Still, it all starts at the time we are saved. Many years ago, John Wesley reminded those to whom he ministered of this truth. I'll paraphrase his words:

> Salvation is not just deliverance from hell or going to heaven; no, while salvation is all that, it is so much more. Salvation is a present deliverance from sin, a restoration of the soul to its initial health, and its original purity; salvation is a recovery of the divine nature; it's the renewal of our souls in the image of God, renewal in righteousness and true holiness, renewal in justice, mercy and truth.*

To be saved is to actually begin the exciting journey of

becoming like Christ himself. It is to begin the journey of holy living.

HOW CAN I EXPERIENCE GOD'S GREAT SALVATION?

Ultimately, salvation is to be experienced. We can know all about it and even realize what God wants to do in saving us; but unless we experience it, all our understanding is for nothing. So, how do we come to find the great gift of salvation that God offers?

It's really quite simple. First, we admit our need to both ourselves and to God. In confessing our need, we start to allow God to work within us. Once we've admitted our need for salvation, we simply talk with God. A prayer we could pray might go something like this: "Father, I have done wrong. I'm sorry. Would You forgive me and help me to change so I can start pleasing You? I want Jesus to be my Savior, and I want to follow Him for the rest of my life. Please help me. Amen."

When we sincerely ask God to save us, He hears our prayer and does for us what we can never in a million years do for ourselves. He saves us and makes us a new person in Christ Jesus. It is the most important decision we can ever make.

How about right now?

Don't run *from* God. Run *to* Him. He offers you salvation in Christ Jesus!

Notes:

*John Wesley, *Wesley's Works,* vol. 8 (Kansas City: Beacon Hill Press of Kansas City, 1986), 47.

Scripture Cited: 1 Samuel 17:36-37; Psalm 18:2; John 3:3; Romans 3:22-24; 8:15-16; 2 Corinthians 5:17, 19; Galatians 3:26; Colossians 1:13

About the Author: Dr. Hodges is senior pastor of Hernando (Florida) Church of the Nazarene.

(2)

SANCTIFICATION

BY KEITH DRURY

Virtually all Christian denominations have a doctrine of sanctification, including Roman Catholics. It is not some weird theological fetish of a few Holiness churches. While many denominations do not speak clearly on *entire* sanctification, the notion of a Christian becoming Christlike through sanctification is so widely accepted that one hardly needs to make an argument for it. Nevertheless, this chapter lays out in basic form the whole idea of sanctification, then explains how Holiness churches (and others) approach the idea of *entire* sanctification.

CONVERSION—AN OUTSIDE JOB

When we are saved, some things happen totally outside of us. Our position changes in heaven and our name is written in the Lamb's Book of Life. These are not inside changes, but things said about us or changes in our position before God. For instance, when we are saved, we are "justified"—declared "not guilty"—in the courts of heaven. Or we are "adopted"—becoming a child of God and joint heir with Jesus Christ. These things are not changes inside our heart, but things that happen outside of us. Some denominations emphasize mostly these "legal" changes of a saved individual and don't talk much about the inside changes. Wesleyan theology also emphasizes the inside changes.

15

CONVERSION—AN INSIDE JOB

Nevertheless, lots of things also happen inside us when we are saved. We are "regenerated," born anew so that we become alive inside; and we are transformed—old things pass away and all things become new. Some old habits fall away immediately and new desires appear in their place: hunger for the Word, the fellowship of other Christians, and the desire to pray. These inside changes are beginning sanctification.

INITIAL SANCTIFICATION

Sanctification begins the moment we are saved. The term describes all the actual changes God makes inside us that make us more like Christ, producing holiness. Holiness is Christlikeness, and sanctification is the term for God's work of making us like Christ. The first great leap we take toward Christlikeness occurs when we are saved. Salvation changes things. It is more than a technical or "legal" change in our position in heaven. It is also an actual change in who we are and what we want. Conversion changes us; this is called "initial sanctification."

PROGRESSIVE SANCTIFICATION

The changes God performs in us when we are saved are not finished. God could make us perfect in a moment when we are saved, but ample evidence show that He does this rarely, if ever. There are still changes we need in word, thought, and deed to become more like Christ. So, God provides us with the "means of grace." The means of grace are the ordinary channels through which God's changing grace flows to make us more Christlike. John Wesley especially emphasized five: fasting, prayer, Scripture, the Lord's Supper, and "Christian conference" (gathering with other Christians intentionally focused on spiritual growth); but there are other classic means of grace, including solitude, silence, suffering, and more.

The means of grace are the ordinary ways God sends changing grace to us to make us more like Christ (assuming we cooperate). God could use the telephone book or golf to change us, but those are not His usual channels. Our job is to get under the influence of the means of grace and let God change us gradually as a Christian, producing progressive sanctification. The old-timers described this as getting "under the spout where the glory comes out." When we go to church, listen to solid preaching, take Communion, read the Bible, and pray, God changes us—if we do not resist His grace. This is called "progressive sanctification," God changing us gradually to make us more like His Son Jesus Christ. It began as soon as we experienced initial sanctification—the moment we were saved. God's progressive sanctification gradually helps us put off unrighteous words, thoughts, and deeds and helps us take on a lifestyle of righteous language, godly attitudes, and holy habits. Over time, we become more like Christ under the influence of these means of grace. All true Christians in all denominations believe in and experience progressive sanctification.

ENTIRE SANCTIFICATION

While progressive sanctification is widely accepted in all Protestant and Catholic circles, the idea of entire sanctification is not as common. John Wesley is known for restoring this biblical teaching of some of our Early Church fathers. Entire sanctification is a powerful work of grace subsequent to conversion in a Christian's life, where God performs a kind of "second conversion" that enables a believer to leap forward in his or her progress toward Christlike living. Some churches today (often called "the holiness churches") especially preach this second work of grace, encouraging Christians to "go on unto perfection" (Hebrews 6:1, KJV).

Most folk today shy away from the term "perfection" because of the way we understand the word. We think it means "beyond improvement" or absolute godliness, but this was not how the Bible's writers understood it. To them, it meant something more like maturity, wholeness, or complete devotion and love of God. What Christian doesn't yearn to be mature and whole and to fully love God? All of us do. Are we left to the gradual process the rest of our lives? Or could it be that God has provided an experience where ordinary Christians can be made full of love for God and others? Holiness churches answer, "Yes."

John Wesley, many church fathers, and today's Holiness Movement teach that God can do this spiritual work by the Holy Spirit. We say Christians who have grown in grace gradually usually come to a place in their journey when they hit a snag. Perhaps they run into a temptation they just can't defeat gradually. Or maybe they discover there are levels of love they just don't have. Sooner or later, most Christians discover there is sin they can't beat and power they don't have. To these folks, the preaching of entire sanctification comes like a rope to a drowning person. The message announces, "You do not need to be stuck forever in a try-and-fail cycle of defeat; you can become what you were intended to be and what God calls you to become." We say that God can change us inside so that we can actually become a fully devoted follower of Jesus Christ, more than a casual Christian.

OUR PART

So, how does a person receive this grace of God that becomes a kind of midcourse correction in his or her journey toward Christlikeness? *By faith*—the same way we become a Christian in the first place. It is not by trying, but by trusting. Only God can fill us with His Holy Spirit. We cannot work our way into His fullness. It is a gift of God. Yet, we do have a part to play—or actually two parts. First is consecration: committing our all to God. Of course, we already did this in an initial way when we were saved; we cast ourselves completely on God's mercy and dedicated our lives to Him. Yet, most of us discover as we grow that we see inside reservations and resistance to God. We *want* to obey and love, yet we often fall woefully short of full obedience and love. It is as if we are only 60 percent committed or 80 percent or even 98 percent consecrated to God, but not 100 percent sold out to God. We seem to be holding back, resisting God in some areas. The solution to this is a decision to surrender all to Him—making a total consecration to God, whatever the price. We offer ourselves a living sacrifice to Him, trusting God with our total self. This is *consecration*—the first part of what we do in seeking entire sanctification.

Our second part is faith: believing God will do what He promised: sanctify us through and through. We believe if God called us to love God and our neighbor with all our heart, He must be willing to actually give us the grace to live up to what He has commanded. We believe that God's commands in Scripture are not just ideals to work toward, but actually possible to reach if we let God change us.

Why do so few receive this work of God? It is the same reason so many are not saved. They either have not heard about it, or they do not believe it is possible. Our unbelief in either case blocks us from receiving this grace from God. Like the city of Nazareth, where Christ's miracle-working power was cut short, Christians today get less from God because we expect less—we have trouble believing God can do so much.

GOD'S PART

If we consecrate our all to God and reach out in faith, God can sanctify us completely, making pure our love and devotion. He can! He may not always do it immediately, but we can seek until we find Him. We don't know why, but some Christians must continue seeking this work for days, months, and even years before God completely sanctifies them. All we know is we are told to keep on asking, keep on seeking, keep on knocking until we receive. God is always faithful to do what He has promised!

IS THERE ANY GROWTH AFTER THAT?

One of the greatest misunderstandings of entire sanctification has been caused by the word "entire." Like the term "perfect," it is taken to mean something so complete that there is nothing more to receive. The notion that a human being could be entirely Christlike so that there is no room for improvement is so repugnant to us that we reject the whole idea completely. And we should. If entire sanctification means entirely Christlike, then the teaching is false and should be rejected. But it does not mean this. So then, what is entire?

Entire sanctification is not an end-product; it is our heart that is entirely sanctified. A person who is entirely sanctified still has plenty of room for growth. In fact, our growth should accelerate! So, what is entire? Our love can be entire. We can grasp that. For instance, a man might entirely love a woman, yet still have lots of room for growth as a husband. He can be fully *devoted* to her, yet still have room to be fully *formed* as a husband. They are, of course, related, for full devotion makes becoming fully formed easier; and conversely, a partially devoted husband is unlikely to ever become fully formed as an ideal husband. Entire sanctification deals with our love and devotion to Christ, enabling us to be completely and wholly devoted to Him, which will then hasten our actually becoming more like the person Christ has called us to be. This, in a nutshell, is the message of entire sanctification.

VARIED APPROACHES TO SANCTIFICATION

While the above description generally describes the official view of many churches in the Holiness Movement, there are a variety of approaches to entire sanctification among Holiness people, and among evangelicals. While arguing over these varied approaches can be divisive and perhaps even useless, it is still worthy to know what the general views of entire sanctification are in the larger Christian community. It will aid informed and sensible discussion. However, we should always remember that we most all agree on the goal—becoming fully Christlike in word, thought, and deed. Here are the seven views of sanctification currently most prevalent in the Christian church. We will use the phrase "becoming a fully devoted follower of Jesus Christ" to mean entire sanctification:*

1. **Seek and receive by faith right now.** Becoming a fully devoted follower of Christ is possible right now—today! Come and receive it now. Consecrate your all to God and receive this second work of grace by faith. Why wait for such a good gift? God will not hold any good thing from you—come and receive. (Historically, this has been the view of the American Holiness Movement as associated with Phoebe Palmer.)

2. **Keep seeking until you receive.** A fully devoted follower of Christ is possible before death or old age, but you cannot experience it just by asking and believing at any moment. God can cleanse and fill you in His own good timing, and, thus, you should keep on seeking until God responds with a second work of grace enabling this life of power and purity. Don't give up, but keep on seeking —it can happen! (Although John Wesley's teaching here is greatly debated, many scholars would contend this was Wesley's view.)

3. **Gradual growth process.** While it is possible to become a fully devoted follower of Christ in this life, it can be achieved only after many years of a gradual process of spiritual growth—putting off sin and put-

ting on deeds of righteousness through Christ's power. By putting to death all sin and putting on a life of holiness through God's grace, you will move gradually closer to Christ. You can eventually—usually after many years—become a fully devoted follower of Christ. Your job now is to follow the Spirit's leading in one area at a time. (This is the generally held position of mainline-denomination Wesleyan theologians, such as Thomas C. Oden.)

4. **A sustainable experience with momentary lapses.** Becoming a fully devoted follower of Christ can be the normative experience in a believer's life as the Holy Spirit enables a believer to suppress the sin nature and live in sustained victory over it. However, because the root of sin remains until death, there will be moments in which sin will cloud or diminish victory. Sin or disobedience is an exception, rather than normative for Christian living. (This is the classic understanding of holiness in Keswick theology.)

5. **A momentary but unsustainable experience.** Becoming a fully devoted follower of Christ can be experienced in moments or short periods of life, but can't be sustained for the long haul. There are times when a believer can truly act out of the complete love of God and the love of neighbor, untainted by selfishness or pride, but the "old man" is too strong to be completely vanquished in life. (This would represent a modern evangelical Lutheran perspective, as seen in the work of Gerhard Forde. Some scholars would argue this was Martin Luther's position.)

6. **Worthy goal but impossible dream.** While it is clearly impossible in this life to ever actually become a *fully* devoted follower of Christ, you should head

that direction anyway, trusting God to deliver you increasingly from sinful thoughts, words, and deeds, and gradually to empower you in love. However, you will never get there; you will never become fully devoted. Total devotion is a journey, not a destination you ever actually arrive at. (This view represents the position of Reformed theology and can be seen in the work of John Calvin, Reinhold Niebuhr, J. I. Packer, and Sinclair Ferguson.)

7. **Holiness of Christ.** All humans—including all Christians—are so sinful at the core that even becoming a *partially* devoted follower to Christ can't be realized in this life. Rather, true Christians should confess our sinfulness and realize that God has imputed Christ's righteousness to us. God can't see our sinfulness, but sees only the holiness of Christ; holiness is about Christ, not us. (While this view enjoys some degree of popularity in contemporary evangelicalism, it has not been held historically by credible and respected orthodox theologians. Some have placed Martin Luther and/or John Calvin in this camp by focusing on their understanding of imputed righteousness. It may be that because Luther, and to a much lesser degree Calvin, focused so much attention on our objective standing before God—and he was preoccupied with it—his understanding of *imparted* righteousness has been missed or inadvertently dismissed by his theological heirs, leading to this perspective today. Luther's primary focus was on justification, but he does address sanctification.)

All of these views can be seen in today's churches. The first two are most common among Holiness churches who preach and teach that God can make us be what He has called us to become. The holiness message is thus optimistic about humans becoming all they were meant to be. It puts great trust in the power of God to perform radical transformation of people like you and me, making us to become what we are called to be—*fully devoted followers of Jesus Christ.*

Notes:

*"Fully devoted follower of Jesus Christ" may not be the best description of the life of entire sanctification, but it is currently most popular, thanks in part to Bill Hybels. This list of seven views was developed with Dr. Chris Bounds, professor of theology at Indiana Wesleyan University.

Scripture Cited: Hebrews 6:1

About the Author: Keith Drury is associate professor of religion at Indiana Wesleyan University and author of *Holiness for Ordinary People.*

SANCTIFICATION—HOW DOES IT HAPPEN?

BY DAVID W. HOLDREN

God calls each of us to be more than merely forgiven. He calls us to become like himself, as we see Him in Christ (see Ephesians 5:1). It sounds like an impossible mission, but it is not, since God does not set us up for failure. The goal of this chapter is to bring together the issues of what sanctification is with how it unfolds in a person's life.

If you are not familiar with the concepts, your mind may be swirling as you ponder the meaning of the salvation and sanctification terms mentioned in this book. As we approach the "how" issue, let's clarify some distinctions between one's salvation and one's sanctification.

HOW ARE SALVATION AND SANCTIFICATION DIFFERENT?

Consider marriage as our analogy, since it is the one used in Ephesians 5. When I got married, my delight was primarily about what (whom) I was *getting*. I claimed this wonderful woman, all for myself. She was mine. She met my criteria and would surely meet my needs and expectations. Do you see a theme here? It is mainly about the great deal *I* was getting.

Initial motives for becoming a Christian often center on the great deal I am getting, at God's expense. He provides the love and grace. Christ did the dying for my sins. God extends mercy and forgiveness to all who believe on His name. I receive eternal life. My past is no longer held against me. I am privileged to receive Christ as *my* Savior. Do you see a theme here? It's all about benefits. Salvation is mainly about the great deal *I* am getting.

If two people in a marriage plow ahead, insisting that all of their own expectations be met, their own needs fulfilled, where is that marriage likely headed?

Marriages that thrive are the ones where each partner eventually realizes the need to make a second kind of vow. It is a deep-level consecration to the marriage and to loving their partner, regardless of effort, sacrifice, and cost. Though many begin marriage as a kind of relational "salvation," its ultimate success depends on a kind of "sanctification." Marriages thrive on eliminating marriage "sins," and developing faithfulness in love and contribution. Living a life that is full of oneself is the surest way to plunder all else around us. So it is in our Christian walk.

As we live the Christian life, we normally become quite aware that a lot of "me" keeps getting in the way of doing what Jesus would have us do. The Bible sometimes refers to the "me" factor as "the flesh," the flawed human nature, the inclination to sin and ungodly character and behavior. The "me" factor needs help (read Romans 7:7-35). Personal sanctification is needed for the Christian life to thrive.

Salvation depends on Christ as our *Savior;* sanctification seeks to establish Christ as *the Lord* of our life.

INGREDIENTS OF THE SANCTIFIED LIFE

The terms "sanctify" and "holy" both come from the same Greek word, which means to set apart or dedicate for God's use. It also has the meaning of being purified, or cleansed for sacred use. That is the often-repeated emphasis in Scripture which is the essence of the holy life, which sanctification brings to pass. Generally speaking, sanctification describes the journey to holiness, which is more the destination, although both remain dynamic in our lives.

In his letter to Timothy, Paul issues the challenge to flee evil and pursue righteousness (see 1 Timothy 6:11). In Ephesians, the admonition is to "put off your old self, which is being corrupted by its deceitful desires; . . . put on the new self, created to be like God in true righteousness and holiness" (4:22, 24). Jesus calls us to be perfect, as our Father in heaven is (Matthew 5:48). In many other terms, phrases, and analogies, the Bible describes sanctification as a combination of deliverance and dedication, all of which happen in partnership with God.

Sanctification addresses the issues of liberation from the power, control, and practice of sin, and the level to which we can arise in loving God and one another, assisted by God's Holy Spirit. Sanctification and holiness orbit around the complementary issues of cleansing and character.

HOW DO WE PROGRESS FROM SALVATION TO SANCTIFICATION?

One theory says that it all happens when a person first comes to Christ, in faith. This writer believes that all things are possible with God, but it is human nature and need that tend to suggest that inviting Christ into our lives as Savior and surrendering to Christ as Lord are two very different issues to address.

You may find terms in this book that seem pretty overwhelming, like *entire* sanctification, Christian *perfection*, perfect love, and even "second work of grace." These have been common terms in Holiness churches (such as The Wesleyan Church and the Church of the Nazarene) for years, but they can be confusing. For example, the term "perfect love" actually refers more to intention than flawless performance. The phrase, "second work of grace" is as much about a deeper commitment level on our part as it is describing what God does.

Holiness is all about being imitators of God, or more specifically, being Christlike. Most Christian sects or denominations have teachings on holiness, but they vary widely in their understanding of the journey to get there and its implications on lifestyle.

Virtually all Protestant groups agree with the need for and pursuit of sanctification. The major area of disagreement has been over the degree to which a person can experience the sanctified life, and how it is attained.

Wesleyan views of entire sanctification are optimistic, to varying degrees. Let's return to the marriage analogy.

At what point is each person in a marriage *entirely* married? It is a fair question, for the sake of marriage and for a discussion of sanctification. Both marriage and sanctification share the notion of a person being "set apart" for specific and holy purpose. It involves a kind of total dedication.

So, when *are* two people entirely married? Is it at the official pronouncement of the marriage by the officials of church and state? Does "entirely married" occur at some mystical moment during the marriage? Or can two people ever be entirely married until their final moments of life on earth? Think about it.

THREE WESLEYAN VIEWS OF ENTIRE SANCTIFICATION

Dr. Chris Bounds, professor at Indiana Wesleyan University, presents an insightful résumé of three basic positions among Holiness churches as to the entirety of sanctification and when it occurs. The following explanations are flavored with the views of this author as well.

First, there is "the shorter way," which is the most optimistic view. This view says that Christians can experience entire sanctification now, in the present moment, in the twinkling of an eye. It comes as we surrender the total self to God; He purifies us from sin and its nature in us, and enables us to love and obey Him with all of our being. This view sees sanctification as mostly an event in which God does most of what happens, and it is complete in that moment in time.

Next is "the middle way." This view suggests that Christians are not able to simply exercise faith at will for God to sanctify the heart and life. We need to have a fairly clear grasp of our need and a growing passion to pursue holiness.

This view sees entire sanctification as being a combination of several things: clear acts of consecration and response, coupled with discipline, repentance, growth, and maturity over time. Sanctification is a partnership where God *and* the individual have clear and distinct responsibility. Sanctification is sustained and built upon over the course of a life that is faithful and utterly responsive to the leadings of God's Word and Spirit.

The "shorter way" distinguishes between Christian maturity and holiness. It holds that a person could be entirely sanctified, yet not be spiritually mature, while the "middle way" sees a stronger connection between maturity and holiness.

Third, there is what may be called "the longer way." This view suggests that entire sanctification occurs in one's life only after a long journey of growth, dying to oneself, discipline, and maturing to the point of truly understanding the meaning of entire sanctification. In this view, Christian maturity is what really makes one ready for entire sanctification. Process is more the focus than an instantaneous event, and setbacks are not uncommon. There is a greater emphasis on suppression of sin than once-for-all-time deliverance from sin. In this less-optimistic view, entire sanctification is more likely to occur shortly before or at the moment of death.

Although John and Charles Wesley both longed for holiness in this life, they disagreed on when and how much of it one could expect here on earth. John was an intelligent and intense man, disciplined and driven. His "shorter way" views of sanctification reflected aspects of his personality. As he matured, he began to wonder if his expectations for the level of deliverance from sin that he taught others was too severe, becoming more of a bondage than freedom. In his earlier years, Wesley preached an entirety in sanctification that was immediate and complete. In later years, he stressed more process and growth in holiness.

Charles Wesley retained a lofty expectation for the level of one's sanctification, but believed that its attainment was only achievable at death.

HOW, THEN, MAY ONE BE SANCTIFIED, EVEN ENTIRELY?

I submit for your consideration that sanctification leading to a holy life flows from four aspects of experience: *discontent, dedication, deliverance, and discipline.* All of this is the interaction of a divine-human partnership, or relationship. Some aspects of sanctification only God can accomplish in us. Some things He will not do for us.

Discontent

As mentioned earlier, people come to Christ out of a sense of need. We need forgiveness from sins committed and we want Christ in our lives and we want eternal life. All of these are valid prompters to come to Christ in faith. We are born again to a new life, focused in a new direction.

However, we have three enemies that are opposed to our new life. They are the world, the flesh, and the devil. By these, we mean the ungodly forms of influence that exist daily in our world; the aspects of our human nature that are bent toward pride and self-centeredness; and Satan, the ultimate personal force of evil in the universe.

Besides this "unholy trinity," we contend with the multitude of pressures from our past and the daily pressures of life. We struggle with impure motives and thoughts. Our words and actions are often far below the most basic expectations for a Christian. It can seem that the harder we try, the deeper in defeat we get. The Christian life is not working out as we had hoped. However, this discontent can give rise to a new day!

At this point, repentance is our ally. Repentance is about taking a good look at the way things have been, and declaring our discontentment. We long for life on a higher plane, doing what Jesus would do. We realize that we have not arrived, and that is not acceptable.

Dedication

Christians talk about "accepting Christ" or "trusting in Jesus" or "receiving Christ." It almost sounds like we are doing God a favor, though it is not intended that way. Rarely is the notion of self-sacrifice or personal surrender to God considered in those early stages of Christianity. We prefer the benefits without much cost. We are bent on "cheap grace": forgiveness without repentance, Christianity without Christlikeness, deliverance without discipline.

At some point, we need to make a clear and conscious shift from a self-oriented life to a Christ-oriented one. Paul puts it this way: "Therefore, I urge you . . . in view of God's mercy, to offer your bodies as living sacrifices, holy and pleasing to God—this is your spiritual act of worship. Do not conform any longer to the pattern of this world, but be transformed by the renewing of your mind" (Romans 12:1-2). This is a call for total dedication and transformation, accomplished as God and we do our parts. You can do that. People around you will be glad you did. God will rejoice. You will know that it was the best investment you ever made!

It is virtually impossible for a marriage to survive when two individuals are determined that the relationship is for the purpose of their own needs being met. When each person in the marriage, at some point, truly consecrates, or dedicates themselves to the other person and to the relationship, only then can the marriage thrive.

We first trust in Christ as our Savior. We eventually learn that God calls us to crown Christ as Lord of our lives. We declare a lifelong "Yes" to what God wants and follow hard after the character of Christ, as His Spirit helps us (see Galatians 5:22-23; 1 Corinthians 13:4-8).

Discipline

Discussions about sanctification and holiness often focus on what God does for us to make us holy. Two outstanding examples of this are when the writer of 1 John says, "If we confess our sins, he is faithful and just and will forgive us our sins and purify us from all unrighteousness" (1:9). And in 1 Thessalonians 5:23, it says, "May God himself, the God of peace, sanctify you through and through. May your whole spirit, soul and body be kept blameless at the coming of our Lord Jesus Christ." These are the things we believe God does.

However, there is a long-underrated secret to a holy life: *self-discipline for God's sake.* Consider only a few examples:

- "For God did not give us a spirit of timidity, but a spirit of power, of love and of *self-discipline*" (2 Timothy 1:7, emphasis added).
- "Let us *purify ourselves* from everything that contaminates body and spirit, perfecting holiness out of reverence for God" (2 Corinthians 7:1, emphasis added).
- "But you, man of God, flee from all this, and pursue righteousness, godliness, faith, love, endurance and gentleness" (1 Timothy 6:11).

Remember, life is a partnership between God and us. So is the Christian life and the holy life. There is one final aspect of sanctification that makes it all possible.

Deliverance

If the sanctified life is one that reflects Christ, then whose help do we need to achieve it? We need the Spirit of

Christ to be at work in us to be holy people. The Lord is the Spirit, and "where the Spirit of the Lord is, there is freedom" (2 Corinthians 3:17).

All of the self-management, self-control, and self-discipline in the world will not lead us to the level of living that can be achieved when we are daily surrendered to and focused on God's Holy Spirit helping our human spirit. The Spirit guides us, prods us, and even cooperates to transform us from the inside out. The outcomes of God's work inside us are partially described in Galatians 5:22-23. Take a look at that wonderful list of character and behavior traits.

ENTIRELY SANCTIFIED?

A holy life is one of consecration, character (like Christ), and contribution. It has been said that sanctification which does not begin with the individual does not begin, but sanctification that ends with the individual ends.

Now returning to an earlier question, when are two people *entirely* married? Is it at the completion of the wedding ceremony? In one sense, the answer is yes. And yet, though completed in the legal sense, it is far from completed or entire regarding growth and maturity. Apart from the attainment of maturity and the saving graces of any good relationship, the marriage will lack fulfillment and even faithfulness. In yet another sense, the marriage is not entire or complete until the final day of that couple before the death of one of them. Then, it is complete.

God's work (grace) is never finished or completed in our lives until we leave this earth. Our holiness is never entire or complete, in one sense, until our final breath is exhaled.

Yet, there is a sense in which we can experience "entire sanctification." It is found in presenting *all* of our self to God (see Romans 12:1); for *all* the days of our life; and learning to love God with all of our heart, soul, and strength, and loving our neighbor as our self (see Mark 12:30-31). It is entire and complete in intention and declaration. Then, we validate that in practice as we daily walk in responsiveness to Christ and the Word of God.

NOW, WOULD YOU PLEASE SUMMARIZE?

God calls us all to repentance and transformation. Sanctification is a term that describes the road to holy living. God calls us each to faith in Christ, and to pursue a life of Christlikeness. We can experience entire sanctification and grow in holiness, as we grasp the need for inside-out transformation, and fully present ourselves to God for that journey. It is a daily partnership.

As we grow in faith and love, we also grow in the hope of God's willingness and power to make possible what at first seemed impossible!

The call is clear. The journey is worth it. The results are good for everyone. Are you willing and ready for the journey?

Scripture Cited: Matthew 5:48; Romans 12:1-2; 2 Corinthians 3:17; 7:1; Ephesians 4:22, 24; 1 Thessalonians 5:23; 1 Timothy 6:11; 2 Timothy 1:7; 1 John 1:9

About the Author: Dr. Holdren is the executive pastor at Cypress Wesleyan Church, Columbus, Ohio. He served for 28 years as a pastor and 8 years as a general superintendent of The Wesleyan Church.

WHAT DOES IT TAKE TO BE A HOLINESS CHURCH?

BY STEPHEN LENNOX

Varying estimates say there are between 15 and 20 denominations in the United States and Canada considered to be "holiness" churches. Researchers determined that these were holiness churches based on their doctrine and history. At the risk of being presumptuous, perhaps there is a better way of determining what it takes to be a holiness church. The church that deserves to be honored with the label "holiness" is the church where people are becoming holy. In order to be that kind of church, three things should be true:

- They teach about holiness
- They model holiness
- They encourage holiness

A HOLINESS CHURCH TEACHES HOLINESS

If people are going to embrace this doctrine, they must first understand it. Making this statement is a whole lot easier than doing it, for it requires, first of all, that we have churches with a strong teaching ministry. The biblical truth on holiness does not rely on a few obscure proof texts, obvious only to those already initiated. It relies on nothing less than the character of God manifested in His unfolding redemptive plan, and is obvious to anyone who takes the Bible seriously.

Biblical holiness preaching must be about more than holiness; it must describe God's marvelous gift of salvation, and must explain how entire sanctification marks the earthly culmination of that gift. This kind of preaching is solid, but it doesn't need to reach the congregation with a dull thud. Peter told his readers that it was the Word of God, shared winsomely, that would not only help them "grow up" in their salvation, but would have them coming back for more (see 1 Peter 2:2-3).

Which view of holiness should we teach? Even when we set aside those views of holiness that prevail in non-holiness branches of Christianity, we still have to choose between three views, all with some claim to be true to the teaching of the Bible and John Wesley. These are known as the shorter way, the middle way, and the longer way. (See the previous chapter.)

Almost since the beginning, holiness people have been arguing about which way is the right way, and that argument continues today. Instead of arguing, I suggest we agree that God can sanctify people in a variety of ways. He is God, after all. When we stop fighting over how, we can join in proclaiming that entire sanctification can actually happen in this life, that God can actually convert our will and our nature by an act of grace. That is the radical good news people need to hear and that holiness churches need to teach, if they are going to really be holiness churches.

In our teaching about holiness, we need to explain what it looks like in action. Here again, the tradition has not agreed on the effects of holiness, some putting greater emphasis on externals like dress, others putting less emphasis here. Wesley had strong opinions about what a holiness person should do, but his bottom line was this: whatever else sanctification does, it allows us to love God with all we are and to love our neighbor as ourselves. Wesley's favorite term for holiness was "perfect love." Jesus called love the fulfillment of the Law (see Matthew 22:37-40). Paul spoke of love as "the most excellent way" (1 Corinthians 12:31). Peter defined spiritual maturity as loving others deeply (see 1 Peter 1:22), and John taught that a relationship with God meant living in love (see 1 John 4:17-18). Whatever else we believe about how holiness people should look and act, we can at least agree and teach that holiness must produce love for God and love for others.

Additional standards for behavior and appearance are not necessarily wrong; every organization needs to establish guidelines for how to appropriately express love for God and others. We must, however, keep in mind the purpose of those standards. Some time ago, I called a water specialist to my home to help me increase our water pressure. He disassembled my water treatment system and flushed the pipes and filter tank with acid and water, removing the rusty sludge that had accumulated. Once everything was clean, he put the system back together. I once again had clean pipes, but clean pipes were not my goal. My goal was the unhindered flow of water; having a clean pipe was just a means to that goal. The goal of holiness is not just a life free from sin, but a life full of love. Love doesn't flow well through dirty lives, so our pipes must be clean; but we dare not teach that all that matters is a pure life. A holiness church must teach what the Bible says about the nature and loving result of holiness.

A HOLINESS CHURCH MODELS HOLINESS

After I had explained entire sanctification to an educated believer from a different background, he asked me, with some skepticism, "Have you ever seen an example of this?" No matter how effectively we teach the doctrine of entire sanctification, unless we also model it, we will not see it in the lives of believers. Holiness churches must be places where my friend's question could find an abundance of illustrations in answer. People will be more inclined to seek it if they can see it. The great success of the late 19th-century holiness revival was due, in part, to the use of testimonies. Personal testimonies of entire sanctification were a regular feature of Phoebe Palmer's magazine, *The Guide to Holiness.*

The power of testimony in producing spiritual maturity is not an invention of the 19th century. God knew all about its power and incorporated testimonies in both the Old and New Testaments to guide us in our pursuit of godliness. When we want to learn about the power of the surrendered life, we can listen to the testimonies of Moses, Joshua, David, Stephen, Paul, Peter, John, and many others. The writer of Hebrews offers a whole chapter of heroes of the faith to encourage his readers to be people of faith. The same writer challenged his readers to not only look back to the past, but to look around them and "imitate those who through faith and patience inherit what has been promised" (Hebrews 6:12). I thank the Lord for the godly examples I have been given, people who showed me what the preaching was about. I was able to tell my Christian brother that, indeed, I had seen holiness with skin on.

Churches should provide regular opportunities for people to tell the story of their journey in holiness. Those who have already been sanctified should be encouraged to share (though their God-given humility may make them reluctant. Also, be wary of those overly eager to testify!). So, too, should those who have not yet been sanctified, but who are fully surrendered and seeking God's blessing, those still on the middle or longer way. Too often in our zeal to promote entire sanctification, we have only given a platform to those who have already "arrived," leaving the rest to feel like second-class citizens. All pursuit of holiness is to be celebrated, no matter how early in the race someone might be.

As well, holiness churches should offer a corporate example of holiness by providing another worldview, or to be more precise, a view of another world. The church ought to be heaven with a street address, an ongoing example of ultimate reality, lived out by real people. When people come into a holiness church, they ought to notice the difference as distinctly as if they suddenly walked into a room where everyone was walking on the ceiling.

The Early Church was accused of turning the world upside down. When people enter a holiness church, they ought to feel like they've been living all week in an upside-down world but have now entered the right-side-up world, the world as it was meant to be. In the wrong-side-up world, people value you for what you can do for them; in here, we value you because you are a child of God. Out there, they use people and love things; here, we use things and love people. In the wrong-side-up world, God's opinions are either ignored or given only lip-service; in the right-side-up world, God's opinions are the only ones that matter. Out there, people consider the church irrelevant; in here, the church is understood to be the pure Bride of Christ. Both through our personal and corporate testimony, the holiness church models what God intended.

A HOLINESS CHURCH ENCOURAGES HOLINESS

No matter how well we teach and model holiness, people won't become holy until they give God permission to make them holy. And they aren't likely to give that permission unless encouraged to do so. Human nature being what it is, and sanctification being what it is, people must be repeatedly challenged to advance. In sermons, Sunday School lessons, Bible studies, private conversations, and every other possible venue, those in holiness churches must often hear the call to be holy as God is holy. The converted must be called to full surrender. The fully surrendered must be called to press on to the crisis of entire sanctification. Those entirely sanctified must be called to continued growth. We understand the importance of inviting people to conversion, recognizing that if you do not ask, most will not respond. The same is true for holiness; it will not happen without a conscious choice, and that choice almost always requires an invitation.

Those who begin that process need encouragement. The writer of Hebrews put it this way, "See to it, brothers, that none of you has a sinful, unbelieving heart that turns away from the living God. But encourage one another daily, as long as it is called Today, so that none of you may be hardened by sin's deceitfulness" (3:12-13). The Greek word translated "encourage" suggests the idea of coming alongside to assist. Those on the way to holiness need those farther along to come alongside for encouragement. They do not need us behind them, pushing them, nor do they need us "in their face," reminding them of all that is left to do. They need companions on the journey, people who will pray for them, counsel them, demonstrate the holiness they seek, and remind them to keep seeking until they find it.

Encouragement toward holiness also requires the holiness church to set holiness as the standard for behavior in the church. I must tread gingerly here, for this point is prone to abuse. More than one person has been drummed out of a holiness church for not measuring up. Sometimes the drumming out took place officially; more often, the person was made to feel unwelcome without a word. Following them out the door were many sensitive Christians who refused to associate with such an unloving church. The last thing I want to do is give license to the loveless and critical. Still, it seems to me that unless we make holy living the standard for behavior, people will ignore all we say about the need for holiness. We can talk about holiness and have great examples of holiness, but if unholy people are allowed to flourish in holiness churches, our inaction will speak louder than anything else.

The New Testament Church expected holy living. A portion of each and every epistle addresses what a Christian ought to be and how to live: "Let us behave decently" (Romans 13:13); "Flee from sexual immorality" (1 Corinthians 6:18); "Do nothing out of selfish ambition or vain conceit" (Philippians 2:3); "Rejoice in the Lord always" (Philippians 4:4); "Let your gentleness be evident to all" (Philippians 4:5); "Do not conform to the evil desires" (1 Peter 1:14); "Rid yourselves of all malice and all deceit, hypocrisy, envy, and slander" (1 Peter 2:1); "Abstain from sinful desires" (1 Peter 2:11). The list could go on for pages more. The church need not apologize for identifying how it expects its members to live.

We may want to rethink the purpose of those standards, however. Most people view standards as rules that people must obey or else they don't belong in the church. That is like defining a dictionary as a large book that makes a great doorstop. You can use a dictionary that way, but that definition hardly describes its purpose. Expectations are given to provide a goal toward which people should strive. To say that a holiness church should make holiness the standard is to say that we should be unapologetic about pointing people toward this goal and using biblical measurements to monitor our progress toward it.

Those expectations should also serve as the criteria by which to choose church leaders. That is, we decide who to put in charge based on evidence of holiness. When I was a pastor of a small church, I was always excited to see someone new begin to attend regularly, but especially if that person had leadership experience, financial resources, and good communication skills. We desperately needed leaders and money, so I was tempted to hurry this person onto the board and into a leadership role. I had standards, only they were shallow and out of sync with the Bible. The criterion I should have been using was holiness.

The key is not just having standards. Every church has some standards, even if the standard is to have no standards. The key is having the right standards. Holy living is not just about having clean pipes, lives free of sin. Holy living is about the unhindered flow of love for God and others. Having love as the expectation means we keep encouraging people to be more loving and don't let them settle for something less. It means we choose leaders based not on their business savvy, but on their devotion to God and how well they love others. It means we don't turn a blind eye when someone in the church treats another harshly, but lovingly correct such unloving behavior. To have love as the goal means we do not determine the success of a church's ministry based on less-important things like attendance, finances, or how exciting the worship service. A holiness church evaluates itself based on whether it is a holy church, and holiness is measured by how much we love God and our neighbor.

CONCLUSION

Calling ourselves a holiness church does not make us one. Neither does having a doctrine on entire sanctification in our articles of religion or being part of the holiness tradition in history. Holiness churches are those that teach, model, and encourage holiness, because this is the kind of church God uses to create holy people. That is the only criteria that really matters—whether people are learning to love God with all their heart, soul, mind, and strength and love their neighbor as themselves. Such people are greatly needed in this world divided by conflict and doubtful that anything can make a difference. Such people are needed to prove to a doubtful Christendom that God still has the power to transform lives. May God give us churches that are truly holiness churches!

Scripture Cited: Romans 13:13; 1 Corinthians 6:18; 12:31; Philippians 2:3; 4:4-5; Hebrews 3:12-13; 6:12; 1 Peter 1:14; 2:1, 11

About the Author: Dr. Lennox is chairperson of the Division of Religion and Philosophy at Indiana Wesleyan University, Marion, Indiana.

GROWING STRONG IN HOLINESS

BY C. S. COWLES

Tiger Woods and I have something in common: we both play golf. That, however, is where the similarity ends. While he is well on his way toward breaking every golf record on the books, my level of play gives new meaning to the word "duffer." What's the difference between us?

Raw talent, for one thing. More important, however, is his nearly masochistic level of self-discipline—a fierce focus that astonishes even his fellow professionals. If there is anybody who epitomizes Paul's "this one thing I do" (Philippians 3:13, KJV) passion, it is Tiger Woods.

If athletes devote themselves to strenuous programs of "strict training," as Paul puts it, and "beat" their bodies mercilessly in order to "get a crown that will not last," how much more ought we to dedicate ourselves with single-minded intensity to gaining "a crown that will last forever" (1 Corinthians 9:25-27)? Can I do less—to borrow the title of Oswald Chamber's devotional classic—than give *My Utmost for His Highest?* "Physical training is of some value," Paul adds, "but godliness has value for all things, holding promise for both the present life and the life to come" (1 Timothy 4:8). Such "godliness" is neither automatic nor easy, but requires purposeful attention to all three of the primary dimensions of our spiritual lives: "spirit, soul and body" (1 Thessalonians 5:23).

PRACTICING THE PRESENCE OF GOD

"Fifteen minutes a day," said our high school Bible Club sponsor. "I challenge you to invest the first 15 minutes of each day in private devotions: 5 minutes in Bible study and memorization, 5 minutes in prayer, and 5 minutes reading a devotional book." Well, I thought I could at least do that—and I did. I soon discovered that 15 minutes was not enough, nor 20, nor even 30. For most of my senior year, the best part of my day was the first hour, the time I spent in personal devotions. I still continue that daily appointment when I am in communion with my Lord and speak to Him "as a man speaks with his friend" (Exodus 33:11); and it has been an anchor in the storm, an oasis in the desert, and a banquet feast for my soul ever since.

This discipline has taught me what we must do to develop our spiritual lives.

First, *we need to listen to God.* The written word is the medium through which the Living Word, Jesus Christ, speaks to us through the testimony of "men [who] spoke from God as they were carried along by the Holy Spirit" (2 Peter 1:21). After the risen Lord explained to the two disciples on the Emmaus road "what was said in *all the Scriptures* concerning himself" and He began to share bread with them, "their eyes were opened and they recognized him." In astonishment, "they asked each other, 'Were not our hearts *burning within us* while he talked with us on the road and *opened the Scriptures to us?*'" (Luke 24:27-32, emphasis added). The Bible is not only the match that ignites the "sacred flame," but the oil that feeds it. There are many valid and important reasons for studying the Bible, but none more so than that "these are the Scriptures that testify about [Jesus]" (John 5:39).

G. K. Chesterton, one of England's most articulate Christian authors, was once asked what book he would choose if he were marooned on a desert island. One would expect that his response would be the Bible. It was not. Rather, he chose *Thomas' Guide to Practical Ship-Building*. If trapped on an island, he wanted a book to tell him how to get off the island and back home again.

So it is with the Bible. Though it is a compendium of many books by multiple authors dealing with a wide variety of subjects, it is the *only* book that unerringly points us to Jesus. As Peter made crystal-clear, "Salvation is found in no one else, for there is no other name under heaven given to men by which we must be saved" (Acts 4:12). Augustine rightly observed that "Jesus is in the Old Testament concealed, and in the New Testament revealed."

My high school Bible Club also introduced me to the importance of Scripture memorization. "I have hidden your word in my heart," says the psalmist, "that I might not sin against you" (Psalm 119:11). There are few spiritual disciplines as challenging and yet as rewarding as a systematic program of Scripture memorization. I am indebted to a Christian friend in high school who not only introduced me to a scripture memorization system, but partnered with me in the program. Each of us carried a packet of individual verses on cards that we would pull out at odd moments of the day and study. Then each week we would quiz each other on them. One of the earliest verses I memorized was: "Like newborn babies, crave pure spiritual milk [of the word], so that by it you may grow up in your salvation" (1 Peter 2:2). Thus, I began to store not only single verses, but extended passages of Scripture in my mind. And I have been drawing from that scriptural memory bank ever since.

Second, *we need to speak to God.* What oxygen is to our physical bodies, prayer is to us spiritually. Frank Laubach, who gained worldwide renown as the founder of the modern literacy movement, kept a lifelong journal of his effort to "practice the presence of God." Before getting out of bed in the morning, he would focus his mind on God. "I compel my mind to open straight out toward God," he writes. He disciplined himself to center his mind upon God every 15 minutes, then 5, and finally every minute. "My will-pressure must be gentle but constant, to listen to God, to pray for others incessantly, to look at people as souls. . . . I can feel the spiritual muscles growing." Gradually, he found that constant focus on God came so naturally that he automatically prayed for every person he talked to or who came to mind or whom he passed by on the street. When the phone rang, he would say to himself, "A child of God is calling me." Toward the end of his busy life, he wrote, "God is so close that he not only lives all around us, but all *through* us."* Well, why not?

Third, *we need the "spiritual direction" of devotional literature.* There is a scene in the film, *Black Robe,* where a Jesuit missionary tries to persuade a Huron chief to let him teach his tribe to read and write. The chief resists, unable to see how any good can come from scribbles on a piece of paper. "Tell me something I do not know," says the missionary. The chief thinks for a moment and then responds, "My woman's mother died in snow last winter." After writing the sentence down, the missionary walks to the other end of the long room where his colleague is working and shows him the scrap of paper. "Your mother-in-law died in a snowstorm?" he asks. The chief, wide-eyed, jumps up in alarm. He has just encountered the "magical" power of the written word.

Through the power of words, we not only revel in the written Word of God, but are inspired by Augustine's *Confessions,* moved by the prayers of Francis of Assisi, helped by Thomas à Kempis's *On the Imitation of Christ,* impelled toward holiness by Oswald Chambers's *My Utmost for His Highest,* stimulated by C. S. Lewis's *Mere Christianity,* and lifted up into "the heavenly realms in Christ Jesus" (Ephesians 2:6) by Charles Wesley's hymns.

CULTIVATING A HOLY CHARACTER

There is nothing—nothing in the world!—more important than that we give careful attention to the cultivation of a holy character. "What good is it," asks Jesus, "for a man to gain the whole world, yet forfeit his soul?" (Mark 8:36). That is why Paul urges us to "put off your old self, which is being *corrupted* by its *deceitful desires*," and "put on the new self, *created* to be *like God in true righteousness* and *holiness*" (Ephesians 4:22-24, emphasis added).

Cultivating the discipline of "true righteousness and holiness" means, first of all, that *we will do what is right all the time, and tell the truth every time.* Then we never have to worry about our actions or words coming back to haunt us. The scariest consequence of even small deceits is the hardening of the heart. It is the kind of moral inversion we see so tragically demonstrated in the scribes and Pharisees who looked Jesus straight in the eye, and yet accused Him of being possessed by "Beelzebub . . . the prince of demons" (Mark 3:22). It is the moral equivalent of vertigo that strikes terror in the heart of pilots flying blind in fog or a cloud: the loss of all sense of up and down.

Second, we must cultivate the *discipline of putting God first* in every area of our lives. Holy living is neither automatic nor easy. It means doing daily battle with "whatever belongs to [our] earthly nature: sexual immorality, impurity, lust, evil desires and *greed, which is idolatry*" (Colossians 3:5, emphasis added). It means swimming upstream against a culture that is "separated from the life of God," a society that has "lost all [moral] sensitivity," and has "given [itself] over to sensuality so as to *indulge* in every kind of impurity, with a *continual lust for more*" (Ephesians 4:18-19, emphasis added). What a scary but accurate description of our hedonistic, materialistic, and narcissistic generation, with its rampant "lust for more" of everything.

Third, we must cultivate the *discipline of treating everybody with dignity and respect.* Paul not only reminds us of the second great commandment, "'Love your neighbor as yourself,'" but adds, "Love does no harm to its neighbor. Therefore love is the fulfillment of the law" (Romans 13:9-10). This means, at a minimum, that we will honor our parents and look after them when they are old; that we will break our addiction to violence by affirming the sanctity of all human life, even the life of the enemy (see Matthew 5:44); that we will respect other people's property, that we will honor and protect their good name; and, finally, guard our hearts from the corrosive toxin of covetousness (see Exodus 20:12-17).

HOLINESS AND "WHOLENESS"

Holiness was a scary word for me in my youth, and rightly so. The Scriptures in many places and many ways warns that "it is a fearful thing to fall into the hands of the living God" (Hebrews 10:31, KJV), whom we know is holy (see Leviticus 11:45). The Bible is full of people who, like Isaiah, cried out when confronted with the holiness of God, "Woe is me!" (Isaiah 6:5).

Thus, it was a great revelation when I discovered that the old English word for holy was *hol*. From that root word has come not only *holy*, but a whole family of related words, such as *whole*, *heal*, *health*, *healthy*, *hale*, and *hearty*. What does it mean to be holy? It means to be freed from the toxin of sin—the consequences of which should strike terror in our hearts!—so that we can be whole and healthy again. This is what Paul had in mind when he prayed, "May God himself, the God of peace, sanctify you through and through. May your *whole spirit, soul and body* be kept blameless" (1 Thessalonians 5:23, emphasis added).

The key to holiness of heart and wholeness in "spirit, soul and body" is found in three tiny but mighty words spoken by Jesus: "If anyone would come after me, he must *deny himself . . . daily* and follow me" (Luke 9:23, emphasis added). First, we must *deny whatever dishonors God and damages our bodies*. "Do you not know that your body is a temple of the Holy Spirit, who is in you?" (1 Corinthians 6:19).

How can we desecrate our bodies by poisoning them with nicotine, alcohol, illicit drugs, and a surfeit of fat-laden, sugar-saturated, and chemically-enhanced food and drink?

There is one thing that all addicts have in common: a first cigarette, a first drink, a first over-eating binge, a first coin pushed into the slot machine, a first click onto an erotic web site link, a first inappropriate touch. Our university invited a specialist in workplace sexual harassment issues to address our faculty. She shared her "Ten Commandments" in dealing with members of the opposite sex. The first commandment was, "Don't touch." The second was, "Don't touch." The third was, "Don't touch," and so on. Her point was that if employers and employees would just keep their hands off each other, and avoid any sort of sexual innuendos in conversation, they would never have to worry about drifting into inappropriate relationships or worse.

If we are already addicted to habits and involved in behaviors inconsistent with God's call to holiness, there is something positive that we can do: we can repent. To repent means that we not only stop doing that which is wrong, but start doing what is right.

Second, we must *deny the good in order to achieve the best.* Chess is an ancient and honorable game. Finding myself in a company of professors and fellow students at seminary who loved to play chess, I couldn't resist the many invitations to play, not only during study breaks but after school and in evenings—evenings that my young wife and new baby were spending at home alone. It suddenly hit me while in a chapel service: "What shall it profit me if I become the seminary's chess champion but lose my wife or flunk out of seminary?" (see Mark 8:36). I repented. I stopped cold. I never played another game of chess throughout the rest of my seminary career, nor for many years after that.

"'Everything is permissible for me,'" says Paul, "but not everything is beneficial. 'Everything is permissible for me'— but I will not be mastered by anything" (1 Corinthians 6:12).

We need to be careful that praiseworthy endeavors, such as getting ahead financially or advancing our careers, do not become obsessive, crowding out quality time that should be spent with the Lord, our family, and in servanthood ministries.

Finally, we must *take care of our physical bodies.* When I was a young pastor in my mid-20s, my physician bluntly told me: "You're well on your way to becoming a fat and sloppy, out-of-shape preacher." That shocked me into cutting back on sweets and fatty foods and taking up jogging, which about killed me at first, but eventually became a regimen that not only energized my body, but my soul and spirit for the next 30 years.

Getting adequate rest is also vitally important. It was Clovis Chappell, a great Methodist preacher of an earlier generation, who said, "The most spiritual thing a tired minister can do is go to bed." For me, that meant not only getting a good night's sleep, but taking at least a full day off each week. Since Sundays were my most demanding days, Mondays became my day of rest. When our children got older, I switched to Saturdays so that we could celebrate as a family together.

We need not only a Sabbath day rest each week, but a mini-Sabbatical every year. A church board was impressed by how organized their new pastor was. In his second meeting with them, he presented an outline of the church program for the coming year. Their mouths fell open, however, when they saw that the pastor planned to be gone the entire month of August for his vacation. They were used to their pastors taking a week off, and maybe even two. But a month? "Pastor, that is all well and good," responded one board member, "but remember that the devil never takes a vacation." To which the pastor responded: "Do you want your spiritual leader to pattern his life after the devil?"

CONCLUSION

The path to growing strong in holiness is clear. We must learn to practice the presence of God through daily private devotions. We need to cultivate a holy character in our daily interactions with others. And we must live whole, healthy lives. If we are diligent about these things, we will "grow in the grace and knowledge of our Lord and Savior Jesus Christ" (2 Peter 3:18).

Notes:

*Frank C. Laubach, *Man of Prayer* (Syracuse, N.Y.: Laubach Literacy, 1990), cited by Philip Yancey, *Reaching for an Invisible God* (Grand Rapids: Zondervan, 2005), 205-7.

Scripture Cited: Exodus 33:11; Psalm 119:11; Isaiah 6:5; Mark 3:22; 8:36; Luke 9:23; 24:27-32; John 5:39; Acts 4:12; Romans 13:9-10; 1 Corinthians 6:12, 19; 9:25-27; Ephesians 2:6; 4:18-19, 22-24; Philippians 3:13; Colossians 3:5; 1 Thessalonians 5:23; 1 Timothy 4:8; 1 Peter 2:2; 2 Peter 1:21; 3:18

About the Author: Dr. Cowles is professor emeritus of Northwest Nazarene University, Boise, Idaho. He is currently an adjunct professor at Point Loma Nazarene University and Azusa Pacific University, both in southern California.

SANCTIFICATION AND EMOTIONS

BY LEON AND
MILDRED CHAMBERS

Often in our daily lives we confuse sin and human nature. We wonder about attitudes that we have or hear others express. We ask, "If I am sanctified, am I sinning if I feel this way?" Or we wonder, "If that person is sanctified, how can he or she have such an attitude?" Often our confusion arises because we are not clear about what sanctification changes in our lives and what it does not.

Some would make the experience of sanctification mean too little. Others, however, would insist upon a perfection that would rob us of our humanity. The experiences of conversion and sanctification deal with the sin problem in the human life, but do not affect normal human conduct. The Holy Spirit works *through* human weaknesses or infirmities; He does not *eliminate* them.

ERRORS IN JUDGMENT

The experience of holiness does not mean that we will not err in judgment. The perfection required is perfection of motives, not perfection of the intellect. In Acts 11:2, the apostles and brethren "contended" (KJV), or differed, with Peter over his eating with the Gentiles. Peter explained that he was directed by a revelation from God to eat, preach, and pray with the Gentiles. Then the same apostles and brethren "praised God, saying, 'So then, God has granted even the Gentiles repentance unto life'" (11:18). The brethren erred, but they had not sinned. Their contention would have hindered the Church, but there was no rebellion against the known will of God. When light came, they walked in it.

Such obedience keeps us sinless and guiltless even when there are errors in judgment that result in misunderstanding. These errors may be stumbling blocks to the one who errs and to others as well. It is possible that they could even keep some unsaved person out of the Kingdom. But there is no sin or guilt in mistakes and errors in judgment. As long as we are not rebellious, are walking in the light and obedient, we are fully accepted children of God.

To say that we Christians who err in judgment have not sinned is not to say that we may be indifferent and will not need to improve. We will lament, grieve, and pray over the errors. While they are not held against us as sins, such mistakes will prevent us being as effective Christians as we might be.

LACK OF HARMONY

The experience of holiness does not mean that there will always be perfect harmony among the Spirit-filled. Paul and Barnabas were "sent on their way by the Holy Spirit" on the first missionary journey (Acts 13:4). At a place called Salamis "John [Mark] was with them as their helper" (13:5). Later, however, Paul refused to take Mark on a second missionary journey. "They had such a sharp disagreement that they parted company" (15:39).

The division was not sin; it was human. There is no evidence of any unkind, ulterior motives. In fact, when Mark later proved himself, Paul wrote, "Only Luke is with me. Get Mark and bring him with you, because he is helpful to me in my ministry" (2 Timothy 4:11). Paul did not let differences cut off fellowship.

There is no sin in misunderstandings and differences of opinions. There *may* be sin in our attitude concerning them.

PHYSICAL PERFECTION

Holiness does not ensure physical perfection. Records of suffering saints and accounts of prayers for healing that go unanswered fill the pages of Christian literature. Dedicated men and women weep because physical limitations keep them from achieving for God as they wish they could.

Paul experienced such a problem. "To keep me from becoming conceited because of these surpassingly great revelations, there was given me a thorn in my flesh, a messenger of Satan, to torment me. Three times I pleaded with the Lord to take it away from me. But he said to me, 'My grace is sufficient for you, for my power is made perfect in weakness'" (2 Corinthians 12:7-9). God did not deliver Paul from his physical problem, but He did promise grace to bear it. God also said the He would be glorified as Paul bore his weakness.

The sanctified person has a body that shows the effects of the fall of Adam and Eve in the Garden of Eden. This body tires, falls prey to diseases, at times functions with difficulty. It may take great physical effort to carry on our work for the Lord. The fact that special effort is required is not a sin. We need not feel guilty. God understands our humanity. Sanctification does not give an extra supply of energy; it does not make us superhuman.

PERFECTION OF WORKS

Holiness does not mean perfection of works or self-discipline. As sanctified persons, we will not necessarily perform perfectly each time we have an opportunity to work for the Lord. Humanity prevents this. In 2 Timothy 1:5, Paul expressed deep appreciation for Timothy's faith: "I have been reminded of your sincere faith." Paul is speaking of Timothy's faithfulness to God, but immediately he gives an admo-

nition: "Fan into flame the gift of God, which is in you"
(1:6). Even with Timothy's faithfulness, he could improve
his service.

It is human to have shortcomings. But it is Christian to
press on, to seek God's grace, and to try to overcome these
frailties of humanity.

TEMPTATION

Holiness does not place us beyond temptation. When
we are saved, our sins are forgiven. However, our experiences
of past sinful life are recorded on the brain in permanent
"memory traces." Scientists have discovered that when areas
of the brain are electronically stimulated, past experiences
can be revived with all the reality of reliving them. In everyday living, a sanctified person will remember past experiences under certain circumstances.

If our sins are forgiven, and our hearts are sanctified
wholly, memories of the past may be a source of temptation
but not sin. The past may be a battleground, but it does not
have to be defeat.

NEGATIVE EMOTIONS

Holiness does not place us beyond the possibility of experiencing negative emotions, such as hurt feelings, impatience, worry, anxiety, and similar emotions. To feel an emotion, even strong emotion, is not sin within itself; it is
human. We must know the motive behind the emotion to
determine its purity or sinfulness. The motive (or attitude) is
an internal state that is the cause of behavior. Values and
goals are products of our motives. Attitudes determine the
behavior involved in reaching a particular goal.

Emotions can help us enjoy or dislike a task. They facil-
itate or impede learning. They influence our interpretation
of another person's behavior, either positively or negatively.
While unbridled emotions can erode our spiritual life to the

point that they can become sin, they need not do so. We need a well-developed, well-balanced emotional life in order to be normal persons.

We differ in our emotional responses. All people are emotional, but no two are alike. A recognition of individual differences is necessary or we will stumble in our understanding of perfect love. These individual differences are genetically and environmentally based.

Paul seemed to have no problem in preaching to the Gentiles, while Peter required a special revelation. Barnabas had no problem in forgiving Mark, while Paul required Mark to prove himself. This would say to us that some people find it easier to forgive and forget than do others. Some people just seem to be nice by nature, while others seem to have trouble even with the help of the Holy Spirit.

Since people differ so greatly in emotional responses and since emotions can be evaluated only on the basis of the underlying motives, we would do well to judge no one. To get "red in the face" cannot be equated with hostile motives, as is so often thought. A person might react quickly, speak sharply, and even flush; but these responses may be the result of humiliation, threat to security, fear, or embarrassment rather than anger. Another person might become pale in response to the same stimulus.

The sanctified may even experience strong emotions. Jesus experienced some kind of strong emotion in Gethsemane. Luke 22:44 speaks of Christ "being in anguish." The original Greek shows the word *anguish* to mean "a conflict or struggle." The agony referred to was mental. It was more than mere physical pain.

Whether a strong emotion is sinful depends upon what occasioned it and how it is handled. It must be kept in mind that emotions may lead to sin if they result in loss of faith in God, if a person's motives are affected to the point of rebelling against God.

Let's take a look at some specific emotions.

Concern. Concern may be defined as caring about something. It is considered a somewhat mild emotion. Everyone would agree as to the place of concern in daily living. Christ in His parable of the unjust steward recognized the legitimate place of concern. The unjust steward was commended and told that those who are concerned and plan for the future are wise (Luke 16:1-8).

Worry. Worry is considered by many authorities to be a mild response to fear. Worry is a common emotion, closely related to anxiety but more mild. This emotion is characterized by a circular thought pattern. The worrier in preoccupation thinks over the problem again and again. Worrying breeds more worry. Fear provokes worry, and worry provokes more fear.

Worry in itself is not sin. Paul was so disturbed (worried) concerning the state of the church at Thessalonica that he could not rest until Timothy was sent to investigate and returned with a good report. Paul said, "When I could stand it no longer, I sent Timothy to find out about your faith. I was afraid that in some way . . . our efforts might have been useless" (1 Thessalonians 3:5).

Worry may result from the guilt we feel because of sins committed. But for the Christian whose sins are forgiven, the fears that underlie the worry are not based upon actual guilt. Therefore, the worry is not sin.

Death is our enemy. It is normal to fear death. A sanctified man may be told that he has a terminal illness. He might go through a period of preoccupation with this problem based upon fear. He might be said to "worry" about the condition. He has not sinned. Naturally, in proportion to the degree that he is able to rise above the fear, worry diminishes.

Anxiety. Anxiety is a strong emotion of apprehension or uneasiness stemming from threat or danger, the source of which may be unidentifiable. In this sense, it differs from fear in that the latter is attached to an identifiable object or event in the environment. As with any aroused state, the physiology of the body is altered, the extent of alteration depending upon the degree of anxiety.

For example, the nerves may be so reactive as to be "on edge," causing us to respond out of proportion to the stimulus. We may jump at the slightest noise. The heart and the breathing rate may accelerate; digestion may slow down or speed up; and even the skin may respond with flushing, pallor, or sweating. All these are automatic reactions when we feel threatened, just like anxiety.

Jesus probably experienced some form of anxiety when He actually faced the "cup." His physiological reaction was sweating, as Luke describes it, "like drops of blood falling to the ground" (Luke 22:44). Yet, Christ did not sin. Once again, sin involves rebellion. A sanctified person who feels threatened may respond with anxiety, but without sin.

Impatience. The sanctified may experience impatience. Impatience is the lack of endurance or long-suffering. Our patience threshold is affected by fatigue, illness, stress, or pressure. In these states, we respond more quickly, are more sensitive to a greater variety of provocations, have less emotional control. A sick or tired person is not a "normal" person. Even though sanctified, our physical endurance and, specifically, nervous endurance are limited.

If impatience is a sin, any degree of the emotion is a sin, even impatience with oneself, which all sanctified have experienced—even if under some other label. Some would seem to think it is all right to be impatient with oneself, but not with others. This is inconsistent. Impatience within itself is not a sin.

Even Jesus grew weary of faithlessness and expressed it strongly: "O unbelieving and perverse generation . . . how long shall I stay with you?" (Matthew 17:17). Patience is a fruit of the Spirit. All the Spirit-filled have the fruit of the Spirit, but not all Christians bear all of the fruit equally. There are degrees of spiritual maturity among the sanctified.

Discontentment. The sanctified may suffer discontentment. This emotion may be constructive in that it may move us to higher levels of action. On the other hand, it may be detrimental when we become preoccupied and can't see beyond our circumstances.

The opposite of discontentment is contentment. Paul said, "For I have learned to be content whatever the circumstances" (Philippians 4:11). Note the word "learned." Contentment does not come automatically with sanctification—that is, not constant contentment with all things. While discontent within itself is not a sin, the sanctified should *learn* contentment. "But godliness with contentment is great gain" (1 Timothy 6:6).

The foregoing discussion of emotions has tried to show the place of such common emotions as anxiety, worry, impatience, and other emotions in the life of the sanctified. The purpose is not to "whittle out" a loophole to let us crawl through, settle down, and enjoy or indulge such emotions. The purpose is to help the sanctified avoid self-condemnation for normal, human conduct. Such condemnation can be detrimental to our spiritual victory.

Remember, we have not sinned as long as our motives are pure and there is no rebellion. Any behavior is sin that is an outgrowth of a sinful motive, whether it be an outward act or an internal emotion. But where the motive is pure, the behavior—whether an outward act or an internal emotion— is not sin.

Certainly, emotions may lead to sin. If the emotion affects our Christian faith to the point that we become rebellious, then the motive is no longer pure. Our goals are set according to our motives. When a motive becomes sinful, then sinful goals will be chosen. Sinful motives and sinful goals result in sinful acts. Thus, emotions may lead to sin.

For example, Martha wanted Jesus to rebuke Mary in order to get her assistance when she was "distracted" with her household tasks. Jesus did not treat Martha's action as a sin. If Martha had indulged her emotions to the point that she wanted Mary humiliated and embarrassed, then Martha's motives would have been changed, her goal would have changed, and Martha would have been guilty of sin. Her emotions would have been based upon sinful motives and, as such, would have been classified as sinful.

Even when emotions are not sin, they can hinder our fruitfulness and can be a stumbling block to us and others. Peter's emotion of fear of the Jews, which separated him from the Gentiles, made him a stumbling block to the Gentiles. They must have wondered why he ate with them one day and would not eat with them the next. But his fear was not sin.

Sanctification does not change the biology of the nervous system, which is basically responsible for the physical aspects of emotions; but sanctification does purify our motives. Sanctification will help us to see the need to strive to develop the emotional control that is possible within the limits of our physical bodies.

The experience of holiness does not prevent us from experiencing strong feeling, but it will save us from being unkind or trying to hurt or get even. Holiness will not keep us from desiring fair play, but it will enable us to carry on even if not being treated fairly. The sanctified person may at times experience hurt, embarrassment, humiliation, or similar emotions; but, by the help of the Holy Spirit, we will walk in the light, return good for evil, and serve God with all our hearts.

The question that we might well ask is whether we really love God with all our hearts and love everyone else as ourselves. If we can honestly answer yes, then we need feel no condemnation.

MATURITY

Holiness does not bring instant maturity. When we are first saved and sanctified, we are just as Christian as the one who is mature in Christ; but we are still infants in Christ.

Peter gives incentive to young Christians. "Like new-born babies, crave pure spiritual milk, so that by it you may grow up in your salvation" (1 Peter 2:2). At the moment of conversion, spiritual learning begins. The infant in Christ, by the help of the Holy Spirit and the Church, must shape new behavioral patterns.

Faulty emotional training, unscriptural beliefs, wrong concepts of faith, the development of a falsely guilty conscience, and many other problems may trouble us throughout our earthly journeys. When we are filled with the Holy Spirit, there is greater impetus to grow. However, when newly sanctified, we have only the potential for spiritual growth. Growth is the development of a lifetime. It is not achieved instantaneously.

BIOLOGICAL DRIVES

Holiness does not abolish biological drives. A majority of the textbooks list hunger, thirst, sleep, and sex among the numerous biological drives. There is no sin in any of these drives. All are necessary for the welfare of the individual and the propagation of the race. There is sin in certain types of behavior in response to the physiological pressures induced by the drives, but there is a Christian way to meet all of the biological drives.

The sanctified will seek to see, taste, smell, and touch what will be to the glory of God, even though we will be tempted to do otherwise. The sanctified will not seek to be aroused for evil.

This was Paul's admonition in Romans 12:1: "Offer your bodies as living sacrifices, holy and pleasing to God." The whole body is on the altar to be used to the glory of God. The drives are not eliminated from the sanctified, but they are kept pure.

SELF-LOVE

The experience of sanctification does not bring an end to loving oneself. It has often been preached that we should not love ourselves. The Bible is very clear that as Christians we will love ourselves. In fact, we cannot be a biblical Christian if we do not love self. "Love your neighbor as *yourself*" (Matthew 19:19, emphasis added). Jesus teaches that love for self is the standard for treatment of others.

Acceptance of self will largely determine our attitudes and behavior toward others. If we have a good self-concept, we will have reason to be at peace with ourselves and with others. We feel significant in the sight of God. We have accepted what we can and cannot do. This will bring peace.

The Christian is in the best possible position to love self and to love others. We can face God without guilt and face ourselves and others without condemnation. There is no need to strike out at others or to blame them. Christian love for self is not selfish, not conceited. It is mentally healthy. Christian love is peace with self and with others. A Christian who feels truly loved of God will love him or herself.

As long as we remain confused about sanctification and human nature, we will not be able to grow spiritually and develop mature attitudes. The experiences of conversion and sanctification solve the sin problem but do not obliterate our normal human conduct or eliminate infirmities. God does promise that the Holy Spirit will help us with these human weaknesses, and that is an attitude which allows us to grow in the Spirit-filled life.

Scripture Cited: Matthew 17:17; 19:19; Luke 16:1-8; 22:44; Acts 11:1-18; 13:2-5; 15:39; Romans 12:1; 2 Corinthians 12:7-9; Philippians 4:11; 1 Thessalonians 3:5; 1 Timothy 6:6; 2 Timothy 1:5-6; 4:11; 1 Peter 2:2

About the Authors: This chapter was adapted from *Holiness and Human Nature*, © 1975, Beacon Hill Press of Kansas City.

THE TRANSFORMATION OF HUMAN PERSONALITY

BY C. S. COWLES

It's not about you.

Those four tiny but evocative words constitute the first sentence and the entire first paragraph of the first chapter in Rick Warren's phenomenal best-seller, *The Purpose Driven Life.*[1] They not only grab attention, but tap into a long and deep stream of Christian spirituality that tends to view human personality with suspicion, if not outright hostility. Not only is it *not* about you, we are told, but *you are the problem.* You are so depraved, so vile, so utterly devoid of anything good or praiseworthy that the most spiritual thing you can do is die. Crucifixion of the self, "ego-slaying," that is what it's all about. As John the Baptist put it, "He must increase, but *I must decrease*" (John 3:30, NASB, emphasis added). Not just decrease, but die!

Thus it was that in my teen years, though brimming with the super-charged juices of life, I earnestly sought to "die out to self." With moist eyes gazing skyward, we sang in college chapel services, "Let me lose myself and find it Lord in Thee; May all self be slain and friends see only Thee." I yearned to be a nobody, a nonentity, a *nothing* for Jesus—a mindless, will-less, personality-less oblong blur—"so that God may be all in all" (1 Corinthians 15:28).

Try as I might, however, I could not quiet another voice that shouted out from my inner-most being: *I am not a nothing! I am not a nobody!* I am something, a somebody, because of Someone who created me, who loves me, and who desires that I live in His presence forever. So, how do we resolve the tension between the self that must die, and the self that refuses to die?

THE GRANDEUR OF HUMAN PERSONALITY

It is true, as Joshua Harris puts it, that "it's not about us; it's about God's glory, it's about his renown."[2] And yet when we ask what it is that brings "glory" and "renown" to God, the answer is not at all what the "theology of self-negation" suggests. If there is anything the Bible makes clear from Genesis to Revelation, it is the surprising truth that, as Hans Kung so eloquently expresses it, "God wills nothing for himself, nothing for his own advantage, for his greater glory. God wills nothing but [our] advantage, [our] true greatness and [our] ultimate dignity. This then is God's will: *[humanity's] well-being.*"[3]

This is precisely the exalted vision of the glory and grandeur that God has vested in human beings, which Paul celebrates in the opening paragraphs of his letter to the Ephesians. We are not the spiders, the "hateful venomous" serpents, the "loathsome insects" that Jonathan Edwards imagined us to be in his famous 1741 sermon, "Sinners in the Hands of an Angry God." To the contrary, the apostle lifts his brush in one hand and the pallet of God's magnanimous grace in the other, and paints for us a picture of who we are "in Christ" that is truly breathtaking.

Before the first galaxies were flung into space, God had us in mind. We are not only greatly loved, but the recipients of His "glorious grace, which he has freely . . . lavished on us" (Ephesians 1:6-8). God created us as free, autonomous, and self-conscious beings in order that we might share in His holiness, His "wholeness." He wills that we be complete, fully alive, and in possession of all the faculties of our unique and infinitely precious personalities.

The astounding truth of the gospel is that it *is* about you! The whole purpose of the regenerative and sanctifying power of the Holy Spirit is not to destroy the personality, but to restore it to its original God-designed fullness. It is to liberate it from the distorting, disfiguring, and ultimately destructive "sinful nature with its passions and desires" (Galatians 5:24). It is God's gracious purpose that, like a butterfly released from the cramped confines of its cocoon, we will gently rise on Spirit-lifted wings until we are "seated . . . in the heavenly realms in Christ Jesus" (Ephesians 2:6).

Why such focused attention on us? Here is Paul's astonishing answer: so that "in the coming ages [God] might show the incomparable riches of his grace, expressed in his kindness to us in Christ Jesus" (Ephesians 2:7). God is going to *show us off* as prime exhibits of His "workmanship," His craftsmanship, His artistry, "created in Christ Jesus [for] good works" (Ephesians 2:10). Perhaps Paul was thinking of the psalmist who exults, "You made [man] a little lower than the heavenly beings *and crowned him with glory and honor*" (Psalm 8:5, emphasis added). Even as the artist is glorified in his or her painting, the sculptor in his or her chiseled marble, and the composer in his or her music, so is God glorified when we become the choice and chosen crown of creation that He intended us to be. Through the indwelling power of the Holy Spirit, we are being "*transformed* into [Christ's] likeness with ever-increasing glory, which comes from the Lord" (2 Corinthians 3:18, emphasis added).

Unfortunately, this exalted vision does not reflect our actual situation as fallen creatures in a broken world. Because of sin's curse, we are damaged goods.

THE HOLY SPIRIT AND PERSONALITY DYSFUNCTION

Psychologists and sociologists are fairly evenly divided between the "nature" and "nurture" schools of personality formation. Our own experience and observation leads us to believe that we are products of both "nature" and "nurture." We are hard-wired with powerful drives that we spend a lifetime seeking to harness and actualize in life-enhancing ways. On the other hand, we are also aware of how fragile and malleable we are, and what a deep impact our families, society, and environment have upon us.

At 10:30 A.M. October 3, 2006, just outside Georgetown, Pennsylvania, Charles Roberts, a 32-year-old loving husband, caring father, and hardworking milk truck driver laid siege to a one-room Amish schoolhouse in his own neighborhood, trussed up and systematically shot 10 girls ranging in age from 6 to 16 before turning his gun upon himself. Four girls died instantly and two more died later. This shocking spasm of violence was an admittedly extreme but not atypical example of the volatility of the human personality.

In the midst of that scene of unspeakable horror, however, a wondrous light of *agape* love burst like a flare in the night sky. Marian Fisher, 13 years old, told Roberts, "Shoot me and leave the other ones loose." This so startled him that he asked the girls to pray for him before proceeding with his dastardly deed, finally turning the gun on himself.[4] "Greater love has no one than this, that he lay down his life for his friends" (John 15:13). It is hard to imagine a scene in which the wildly different potentialities of human personality were put in sharper juxtaposition than that.

Life and Death Instincts

Two compelling and contradictory drives, bubbling up like lava from the unconscious, are ever at work in the human psyche: the life and death instincts. The robust will to live, shared by all animate creatures, expresses itself through powerful aggressive and defensive mechanisms. A baby is born with a strong set of lungs that can disrupt a whole household until its urgent needs are met. Likewise, we do not have to give thoughtful consideration as to what action we should take when a semitruck suddenly pulls out in front of us: our bodies automatically react for us.

Because of the sin-warp in human personality, however, the "will to live" conflates into the "will to power." We want not only to survive, but to dominate, to control, to bend everybody and everything to our will. That which cannot be subdued and subjugated must be eliminated. Life becomes death. Frustrated when he didn't get what he wanted, Cain rose up and slew Abel. And we have been killing one another with a vengeance ever since.

The Pleasure Principle

We naturally do that which feels good and avoid that which causes pain. The problem arises when we compulsively pursue pleasure at the expense of everyone else and all other considerations, the destructive consequences of which are on graphic display all around us. The reckless pursuit of pleasure has dethroned kings, disgraced politicians, and destroyed pastors—not to mention its poisonous effect on health, interpersonal relationships, and society at large.

What is striking is that the pleasure principle seems to be just as fiercely operative in the destructive instincts as in the life ones. How else are we to explain our fascination with and addiction to violence in the media, sports, entertainment, and warfare? There is nothing so calculated to focus the mind, stir the emotions, and inflame the senses as a good fight. While the killing of human beings may initially provoke revulsion, it can transmute into an intensely pleasurable experience akin to a sexual climax.

In her searing account of her miraculous survival of Rwanda's 100-day spasm of internecine genocidal violence in the spring of 1994, in which the majority Hutus slaughtered over 800,000 Tutsis and Tutsi sympathizers, Immaculee Ilibagiza reports that a party atmosphere of laughter, singing, and dancing accompanied the killings.[5] Jesus said, "From within, out of men's hearts, come evil thoughts, sexual immorality, theft, murder, adultery, greed, malice, deceit, lewdness, envy, slander, arrogance and folly" (Mark 7:21-22).

Deep Cleansing

In the crisis experience of entire sanctification, the toxin of inherited depravity that has poisoned the well of our instinctual personality is washed away in a cleansing flood-tide of God's self-giving and self-sacrificing *agape* love—a transformative love that is "poured . . . into our hearts by the Holy Spirit" (Romans 5:5). No longer do we pray, "*Mine* is the kingdom, the power, and the glory," but rather "Not *my* will but *thine* be done" (Matthew 26:39, KJV, emphasis added). Instead of the narcissistic pursuit of pleasure, we yearn to "*please [the Lord]* in every way: bearing fruit in every good work" (Colossians 1:10, emphasis added).

Even as darkness vanishes before the rays of the rising sun, so do our dark instincts evaporate in the warm glow of Spirit-generated love. "Blessed are the peacemakers," said Jesus, "for they will be called sons of God" (Matthew 5:9). Like our Lord who "when he suffered, he made no threats" (1 Peter 2:23), we would rather be wounded than wound, would rather suffer pain than inflict pain, and would rather die than kill.

"Do nothing out of selfish ambition or vain conceit," counsels Paul, "but in humility consider others better than yourselves. Each of you should look not only to your own interests, but also to the interests of others" (Philippians 2:3-4). We seek not to dominate but liberate, not to diminish but enhance, not to destroy but enrich. As Francis of Assisi so eloquently put it,

For it is in giving that we receive,
In forgetting that we find ourselves,
In pardoning that we are pardoned,
And in dying that we are born to eternal life.

THE HOLY SPIRIT AND INTERPERSONAL CONFLICT

Even before someone gave me Thomas à Kempis's devotional classic, *On the Imitation of Christ,* I longed to be like Christ. My favorite hymn during my teen years was:

I have one deep, supreme desire,
That I may be like Jesus.
To this I fervently aspire,
That I may be like Jesus.

I assumed that this implied a specific spiritual personality type. And yet as I looked around at the most Christlike people I knew, their personalities were all over the map. Some were outgoing and others timid. Some were voluble and others quiet. Some had a great sense of humor and others not.

It became obvious that there was no single cookie-cutter-Christian personality type. The God who created over 300,000 different species of beetles likes variety. And when He created each of us, He broke the mold. He threw the pattern away. Never before has there been and never again will there be anyone quite like us. Each of us is, truly, one of a kind.

Personality Characteristics

Drawing upon the groundbreaking work of Sigmund Freud and Carl Jung, the Myers-Briggs Type Indicator is one of the most widely used instruments today in identifying and categorizing personality types. Their tests are widely used in the educational, business, and behavioral science professions, and even have been adapted by churches.

The Myers-Briggs system is built on four basic paired extremes of cognitive styles. They are extrovert-introvert, sensing-intuitive, thinking-feeling, and judging-perceiving. These, in turn, combine and interrelate to form 16 personality types that can be identified, measured, and categorized through various testing instruments. If a job applicant, for instance, tests out to be timid and overly sensitive, he or she would probably be ill-fitted for the rough-and-tumble world of real estate sales. Likewise, an entrepreneurial extrovert would go crazy cooped up in a cubby-hole office doing data entry.

The Lord of the Church, who has bestowed "different kinds of gifts" upon individuals and orchestrates them "for the common good" (see 1 Corinthians 12:4-7), also weaves different kinds of personalities into the tapestry of Kingdom work. The quiet and self-effacing couple who faithfully taught primary children in the Sunday School in the church basement for nearly 50 years were just as important in the work of the Kingdom as any who served as their senior pastors.

Tensions

The downside of having so many beetle species is that they are constantly at war with one another, fighting for food, defending against encroachment, and even eating one another. Something like this occurs in every human community, large and small. Variety may be the spice of life, but it also creates innumerable opportunities for discord. When different personalities rub up against each other, friction is generated. It seems to be true that where two or three are gathered together, sooner or later there's going to be a fight. Conflict is endemic to life.

In *The Liar's Club*, Mary Karr relates that her uncle did not speak to his wife for 40 years after a fight over sugar. He even sawed their house in half, moved his half to the other side of their property, and nailed up planks to cover the raw sides. In *Love in the Time of Cholera*, Gabriel Garcia Marquez draws a portrait of a marriage that disintegrates over a bar of soap.[6] I know a devout elderly couple, retired missionaries, who have cut off all communication with their youngest daughter since she got divorced and remarried 20 years ago. They will not speak to her when she calls, and return her cards and letters unopened. Churches have split over drum sets, the days of creation, and the color of carpet.

The Holy Spirit as Healer

A vast array of psychological, sociological, and medical data could be assembled to underscore the truth of Peter's almost off-handed statement: "Love covers over a multitude of sins" (1 Peter 4:8). When it comes to healing the deep dysfunctions of human personality and broken relationships, there is no wonder drug, no psychoanalytic therapy, no sociological program that can touch "the fruit of the Spirit" that Paul lists: "love, joy, peace, patience, kindness, goodness, faithfulness, gentleness and self-control." To which he adds playfully, "Against such things there is no law" (Galatians 5:22-23).

It is against the dark backdrop of Rwanda's demonic holocaust that we see two stellar examples of the transformative power of the Holy Spirit. The first is a Hutu Protestant pastor who, at great risk to himself and his family, hid Immaculee and five other Tutsi women in a four-foot-by-three-foot bathroom just off his bedroom for three months. His home was invaded and searched by Interahamwe killers numerous times. Immaculee believes that God blinded their eyes to the bathroom door hidden behind a large wardrobe. If they had been discovered, not only would the women have been cut to pieces, but the pastor and his whole family as well. Pastor Murinzi exemplified the self-giving, self-denying, and self-sacrificing "greater love" that is the essence of holiness.

The second is Immaculee herself. When she realized that none of her family could possibly still be alive, she began to earnestly pray, "Please open my heart, Lord, and show me how to forgive." God answered her prayer. Her anger drained away, and she began to pray that the killers would be touched with His infinite love. "That night I prayed with a clear conscience and a clean heart. For the first time since I entered the bathroom, I slept in peace."[7] The cleansing of her heart from all hatred and desire for vengeance was so deep that when she later met the man, now awaiting trial for having hacked over 400 Tutsis to death, including her mother and brother—a once proud and handsome Hutu family friend, but now a broken and sobbing wreck crumpled on the ground at her feet—she reached down and touched his hands lightly and said, "I forgive you."[8]

No amount of psychotherapy, personality adjustment, or marriage enrichment seminars can bring about that kind of transformation; only the purifying of the heart by the Holy Spirit, and the continual cleansing "from all sin" that occurs when we "walk in the light, as he is in the light" (1 John 1:7).

Notes:

1. Rick Warren, *The Purpose-Driven Life* (Grand Rapids: Zondervan, 2002), 17.

2. Collin Hansen, "Young, Restless, Reformed" (*Christianity Today*, Sept. 2006), 34.

3. Hans Kung, *On Being a Christian*, Edward Quinn, trans. (Garden City, N.Y.: Doubleday, 1976), 251.

4. *The San Diego Union-Tribune*, Oct. 7, 2006, A1.

5. Immaculee Ilibagiza with Steve Erwin, *Left to Tell: Discovering God Amidst the Rwandan Holocaust* (Carlsbad, Calif.: Hay House, Inc., 2006), 77ff.

6. Related in Philip Yancey, *What's So Amazing About Grace?* (Grand Rapids: Zondervan, 1997), 97-98.

7. Yancey, 92-94.

8. Yancey, 204.

Scripture Cited: Psalm 8:5; Matthew 5:9; 26:39; Mark 7:21-22; John 3:30; 15:13; Romans 5:5; 1 Corinthians 15:28; 2 Corinthians 3:18; Galatians 5:22-24; Ephesians 1:6-8; 2:6-7, 10; Philippians 2:3-4; Colossians 1:10; 1 Peter 2:23; 4:8; 1 John 1:7

About the Author: Dr. Cowles is professor emeritus of Northwest Nazarene University, Boise, Idaho. He is currently an adjunct professor at Point Loma Nazarene University and Azusa Pacific University, both in southern California.

THE MORALITY OF HOLINESS

BY MARK HOLMES

They had worked together on the project for several months, requiring them to spend far more time together than they had anticipated. In the course of their work, they had come to know each other well, as conversations often led toward family issues, individual feelings, and dreams. He had sensed a loneliness within her caused by the indifference of a 20-year-old marriage and the emptiness left by children leaving home. He knew how she felt, the same loneliness gnawed at him. If only he had known her 20 years ago, how different their circumstances would be. But it is too late now, or was it? They both had spouses and families to whom they were responsible. Still, why shouldn't they be happy together? After all, life is so short, why spend it being miserable? No one would know except them. Maybe they could talk about it over dinner tonight instead of going home.

A car pulls up in front of a large building in the city. The man behind the steering wheel turns off the motor while the woman seated next to him nervously chews her lower lip. Sensing her hesitation, the man begins, "Look, we've been over this a hundred times. We both agreed that we are not ready to be tied down with a child. You have your degree to finish, and I need to put my full energy into my job if I ever hope to earn enough money to raise a family. It will be fine. I'm going to be with you all the way." Blinking back tears, the woman hesitantly reaches for the door handle and opens the door. She steps out onto the sidewalk and goes into the building, with the man following behind her.

Tom had always been a night owl, preferring to stay up late while his family went to bed. He had always seen it as "his" time, when he could pursue private issues without being disturbed by the kids or his wife. It was probably the most productive time of his day, as he often made progress on projects he brought home from the office. It was also a great time to get on the Internet and surf his favorite spots. But his interests had changed recently. What once was NASCAR, hunting, and fishing were now web sites about pornography. Initially he felt guilty, but then he decided it really wasn't affecting anyone. It was just between him and his computer. There really wasn't anything wrong with it, as no one was getting hurt.

Bill sat by the hospital bed, holding the nonresponsive hand of the woman he had married 52 years before. They had spent the last two years in this same way: she lying comatose and breathing by the assistance of a respirator; he listening to its rhythmic sounds as it maintained her life. He used to spend this time sharing with her his memories of their life together. But now, he mostly sat and worried how he was going to pay for her care. The two years had succeeded in depleting their life savings. He would have to sell the house. *Why did she hang on so long?* The thought made him shudder with regret for even thinking it. Still, there was the reality that her care was costing more than he could afford, and she obviously was not enjoying her life in this state. If only he could find a way to allow her to die, she would no longer suffer, and he could get on with his life with what little he had left. But wouldn't that be murder?

As you read these scenarios, what was your inner response? Did you feel more strongly about the ones with which you disagreed? Where were they wrong with their decisions? What makes you sure they were wrong? What makes you sure you are right? Experience reveals there is a right and a wrong response to every situation in life; we just cannot agree on how these apply in each situation.

This chapter deals with the topic of morality, or more specifically, the morality of holiness. It is a topic that wrestles with the question of what is right and what is wrong, and how we make the determination. Defining morality through the concept of holiness adds a decided slant to the topic. So, before we jump into holiness, let's first determine what we mean by the word *morality* in general. To do this, we need a brief lesson in ethics.

MORALITY IS OUR MEANS TO AN ETHICAL END

Ethics attempts to answer the question: What is ultimately good for humanity? When we talk about an ultimate good, we mean the greatest possible quality that can be experienced by the greatest number of people. Ideally, the ultimate good would be a universal experience producing the utmost benefit. Morality is the way through which this ultimate good is achieved. Thus, ethics seeks the universal end while defining the moral means of achieving it.

The quest for this ultimate good and its moral means is a challenge, as any attempt to define either of these is soon contested. We all seem to have varying views on the topic. Nations conflict with nations around the globe as each one believes the greatest good will assume their control. Within each nation there are regions, nationalities, and special interests, all with their own opinion of what would work for their best. We are not in want for opinions of what is good, and how to attain it.

THE ERROR OF INDIVIDUALISM

Perhaps the greatest challenge to exercising a morality that will produce a universal good today is found in the shift over the last century, which places emphasis upon the individual instead of the group. Increasingly, we believe each person is unique, and therefore, our individual circumstances require special consideration. In place of pondering the *universal* good, we seek for the *individual's* best. Ethics has become personalized, and in doing so, relativized to each individual's desire and definition.

This individualized influence upon ethics also affects our definition of morality. If I have the ability to define my personal, ultimate good, then I need the right to determine what morals I will exercise to achieve my goal. This may sound good logically, but it develops a position that is nearsighted at best. We have come to the foolish idea that if each individual seeks his or her own good, the sum of these attempts will add up to the ultimate good. After all, if everyone is happy, would that not be the ultimate experience of the good?

Happiness could well be a sign of achieving the ultimate good; however, for this to happen, each person's pursuit would need to contribute to the fulfillment of every other person's good on this globe. Any negative influence one's actions would have on another person's life would automatically discount another's goal or means as being appropriate. Many of the social issues that we wrestle with today are the results of individualized choices clashing with those around them. That which may bring about one's defined good, will probably bring about a negative experience for others. If a "good" is only beneficial to certain people at the expense of others, can it really be considered as ultimate?

Our attempts at individually defining what should be done and how it should be achieved fall apart due to conflict that does not allow for universal pursuit. The mother contemplating abortion most certainly has a different goal and means toward happiness than that of her unborn baby. Her choice to abort cannot be for the baby's ultimate good. Yet, we demand for the right of one to override the other.

My wife works in a hospital as a nurse. Several years ago, while administering a medication, she accidentally stuck herself with the syringe that she had used on the patient. Because of the lady's lifestyle, the potential of her having HIV was high. However, in an attempt to provide patients with a level of confidentiality, the law does not require the patient to disclose whether they know that they have HIV or to be tested to rule it out. The patient can and did refuse to provide any information for my wife. What was designed for a personal good for one, became a nightmare for my wife and our family until we were able to rule out the virus by other means.

Experience proves that any definition of an ultimate good for humankind is not going to be achieved through individual determination. We simply lack the ability and motive for such a grand endeavor. Our focus turns inward. Our ethical and moral compasses are too distorted by our sinful nature. Yet, this does not prevent us from seeking our goal through individual freedom, no matter how distorted our efforts become. We fail to see the paradox between freedom and restriction. We errantly believe that the means to our ultimate happiness as individuals is to exercise our freedom and demand it at every occasion. Yet, we know from our own experiences that the open pursuit of freedoms results in enslavement to the very things we desire. However, if we choose to be restricted by something greater than our personal desires, we discover a freedom that can be obtained by no other means. Thus, according to Jesus, saving our life will result in losing it. Surrendering our life to Him finds it (see Matthew 10:39). Our society appears blind to the reality that the morality we are presently defining has become less effective at achieving the good we desire, which leaves us with a frightening question. Is it possible that we might succeed in developing a morality that will eventually destroy us?

HOLINESS IS THE ULTIMATE GOOD FOR HUMANKIND

So, what are our options? First, we need to recognize that the ultimate good is not the sum total of our individual desires. Instead, our individual good must be the reflection of what is ultimately and universally good. The flow does not move from the individual toward the ultimate, but rather from the ultimate to the individual. In this, we do not define what is good, but rather the good defines us. Thus, the ultimate good for all humankind is holiness as defined by God, achieved through the morality revealed by God. This brings us to the topic of this book—holiness, and the subject of this chapter, holy morality.

Without complicating the issue, holiness can be defined as loving God with one's entire heart, mind, and soul and our neighbor as our self (see Matthew 22:37-40). It is the state of complete surrender to the fullness of God in one's life. Because God is ultimately good, He can do nothing but what is ultimately good. His desires for us must, in turn, be what is ultimately good for each of us individually and all of us universally. His moral directives for obtaining this good would be mutually beneficial for both those who follow them, and for those who experience the secondhand effects of this morality. As Emanuel Kant once said, "The universal end of [humankind] is the highest moral perfection."*

Holiness is both a state that we achieve (the good) and the means by which we attain it (morality). Anything that detracts from this is immoral. Thus, having the ultimate good defined by God provides an understanding of how it is achieved. Yet even in this presentation, we find the challenge of knowing specifically how to live out this moral expression.

It may seem odd to define holiness in terms of a rela-

tionship. We are accustomed to it being defined more by
what we do. Some have understood holiness as the state one
achieves by living a clean life through the observation of
rules. Morality becomes nothing more than the expression of
a moral code. Nevertheless, the pursuit of holiness not only
demands an answer of *what* we do, but also *why* we do it. To
see holiness as merely the purifying of one's character blinds
us to the broader will of God for our lives. He wants us to be
holy, not just to make us good but to enable perfect fellowship between us. In holiness, our relationship with God is
made complete. Therefore, the ultimate good for humankind
is to relate perfectly with God through a perfect relationship.
Anything that promotes and strengthens our relationship
with God can be seen as moral. Anything that diminishes
our relationship with God is immoral.

Because holiness is relational, our pursuit of it can never
be understood as individual. What we do, even when alone,
affects the other participants in our relationships—namely
God and our fellow humans. Thus, the question that guides us
morally is not how will my decision affect me, but how will it
affect my relationship with God and my fellow humans?

HOW DO WE DEFINE A HOLY MORALITY?

So, how do we determine the appropriate moral expressions that make holiness possible? Historically, we have approached this question by several methods.

First, we believe that by understanding the facts that
surround our experiences, we can define how one should respond. The Church has a long history of meetings and de-
bates through which various challenges in life have become
understood. Science and technology are prolific at producing
difficult questions demanding answers, such as cloning, stem
cell research, and other procedures that manipulate life. Each
of these reminds us that ability is not the same as propriety.
It is often easier to present the questions than it is to provide

the response. This approach is not without weaknesses. There is always the risk that we will not fully understand the issue. We might have made the wrong observations, or failed to attain all the necessary insights. As a result, our morality does not take us to the ultimate level we believed it would.

Second, we establish a list of ironclad rules to follow, by which we measure every possible scenario. Here, the general observation rules over the specific expression. However, before long, we discover that there are some circumstances where keeping the rules actually plays havoc with the good. This is illustrated when Jesus healed the man with the withered hand on the Sabbath (see Mark 3:1-6). The good that He did for the man was denounced, because in so doing, Jesus broke the religious rules of the day. Ironically, keeping these rules would have prevented the good. The weakness of this approach is revealed in our inability to regulate a universal morality.

A third attempt we pursue in determining what is moral is the intuitive approach, where the right and wrong of something becomes more of a sense or gut feeling. We may not be able to explain why, but various options in life bring with them a sense of appropriateness or danger. While we can become sensitive to the moral code of God's universe in this way, the subjectiveness of feelings can become confused with our fallen and selfish natures. Our morality eventually reflects more of our image than God's.

Where used alone, these attempts at defining the moral means toward holiness may be limited. In combination, they provide a type of check and balance that overcomes their weaknesses. God, in developing a relationship with us, uses a mixture of each method, infused with His influence, which helps us to determine our appropriate moral expressions. Therefore, as creation was designed with a certain moral code governing the way it functions, observation of this code can help define our actions to align with it. Then there are the rules that God has given through His Word that speak specifically to His will for our attainment of moral completeness. Finally, God has provided for us the direction of the Holy Spirit, who provides personal counsel and influence for our understanding of morality in this life.

The defining and pursuit of humankind's greatest good has long been an object of debate and controversy. Not because it is impossible to determine and experience, but because we fail or refuse to embrace the call and provision of God by which it can be attained. Many have viewed God's concept of holiness to be restrictive and impossible, where it really is liberating and available to anyone wise and brave enough to look beyond his or her immediate experience to the larger truth that defines and fulfills us all.

Notes:
*Emmanuel Kant, *Lectures on Ethics,* tr. by Louis Infield (Indianapolis: Hackett, 1963), 252.

About the Author: Rev. Holmes pastors The Wesleyan Church in Superior, Wisconsin.

LIVING OUT HOLINESS IN EVERYDAY LIFE

BY ERIC FORGRAVE

Most of us have experienced the kind of subtlety people use to hint at something they want us to do or to stop doing. "This garbage smells!" might be translated, "Take out the trash." "Remember our deadline is approaching soon," might be translated, "Your reports need to be done ASAP!" "Want a piece of gum?" might be translated, "You need a piece of gum—your breath stinks." "This room is a pigsty," might be translated, "Clean your room!" Actually, some of those aren't so subtle. People often use subtlety in the hope that we will get the hint, and sometimes it is even a form of manipulation and control.

Subtlety is one of the enemy's best weapons in that sense of manipulation and control—in the sense of stealth, camouflage, and disguise. The enemy uses subtlety to fly under the radar undetected, to sabotage, and to attack. In fact, the kind of subtlety the enemy uses is deadly, like the subtle adjustment of temperature with the proverbial frog in the kettle. The enemy uses subtlety to get a foothold and to outsmart us however, wherever, and whenever possible. This shouldn't be surprising. It has been one of the enemy's tactics since Adam and Eve, and it has continued on through since the Early Church.

This doesn't mean we should spiritualize everything as an enemy attack. Much of the subtlety of sin slips by us because of our human weaknesses. Half-truths, justification, rationalization, and ignorance allow subtle sins to creep into our hearts and lives. We are far more susceptible and vulnerable to self-deception than we realize, and far more prone to miss our blind spots than we want to admit. The psalmist picks up on the dilemma. "Who can discern his errors? Forgive my hidden faults. Keep your servant also from willful sins; may they not rule over me" (Psalm 19:12-13). Subtle sins may not be the big, obvious, overt sins (whatever those are), but they are just as deadly and destructive.

FULL SYSTEM SCAN: DETECTING SOME SUBTLE SINS

If your computer is anything like mine, then the computer's virus protection software alerts you when a full system scan is overdue. The scan is intended to search, inspect, and examine every file and nook and cranny of your computer for unwanted viruses, spy-ware, and for anything else that is a threat to the system. Those kinds of threats are the computer's enemy and can easily cause a system slowdown, shutdown, or complete meltdown. My guess is that many of us know that by firsthand experience. My software seems to take an abnormally long amount of time for this scan, so I usually ignore the first several alerts. Dangerous? Maybe. But it is not as dangerous as letting our hearts and lives go unchecked or unscanned; not as dangerous as ignoring those alerts in our spiritual journeys. If we are willing to keep our computers safe and protected from harmful viruses, however reluctantly, how much more should we be willing to guard our hearts and let God inspect them for deadly subtle sins? The implied answer to that question is, of course, that we should be far more willing to do whatever it takes by God's grace to keep our hearts and consciences clear before God.

Subtle sins can take on innumerable forms and expressions in the lives of believers and can be as specific and

LIVING OUT HOLINESS IN EVERYDAY LIFE   87

unique as each individual, so an exhaustive list is impossible. Hence, the following examples of "subtle sins" are simply meant to stir and sensitize our hearts to the scanning process and the deadly danger and sabotage of sin.

EMPTY WORDS ARE LIKE EMPTY CALORIES

My favorite drink is Mountain Dew. It is my "breakfast of champions." It is my morning coffee or cappuccino. I know there is nothing nutritious about it and that it does me more harm than good, but I like the taste of Mountain Dew. I am probably addicted to the caffeine. OK, I *am* addicted to the caffeine. When pushed on how unhealthy it is, I like to justify drinking Mountain Dew by pointing out that the third ingredient is concentrated orange juice. (It's true! Check it out.) "I'm getting my Vitamin C," I say. In the end though, I know that Mountain Dew is little more than empty calories that only promote accelerated tooth decay and weight gain.

Some of our seemingly harmless words are just as unhealthy and destructive for us and for those we share them with as Mountain Dew is for me to drink. We may think these words are not mean, but they are nevertheless malicious in that they are often unnecessary, at the expense of others, and tainted. In term of having what is good for us or others, they are "empty" words. It's just that we like their "taste"; such words make us look good or get a few laughs. We are probably addicted to the "caffeine" too; that is, we think these words build up our importance. Paul gives a good beginning list of these empty words in Ephesians. "Do not let any unwholesome talk come out of your mouths, but only what is helpful for building others up according to their needs, that it may benefit those who listen. . . . Get rid of all bitterness, rage and anger, brawling and slander, along with every form of malice" (4:29, 31). "Nor should there be obscenity, foolish talk or coarse joking, which are out of place," (5:4).

Don't skip over these verses of Scripture too quickly. It is easy to dismiss these examples of empty words categorically and unconditionally as something we don't have a problem with. It is easy to overlook any or all these unwholesome ways of communicating as rookie mistakes or baby-Christian struggles, but quickly dismissing something as "not a problem we have" can be one of the subtle ways the impairing effects of sin impact our lives and relationships. For example, we might be quick to point out that we never use those well-known, obscene "four-letter" words, but do we unleash words of hate and anger in our hearts while keeping a smile on our face? We might be quick to reason that we never smear and slander someone's good name in public, but what about in personal conversations over lunch, at the water cooler, among a few close coworkers, or on the phone? We might be quick to defend our ways of taking jabs at people as harmless sarcasm, but do we really do it to show them up, to spite them, to try to get them worked up, or to make ourselves look good? Do we realize that others might take our sarcasm the wrong way, even though that may not be our intention? We might strongly deny maliciously gossiping about others, but there is no denying that gossip is a plague that chokes the unity of the Church. We might be quick to justify the ways we joke around as *just* joking, but if we have to justify it, then something is not right. Behind the smokescreen is a way of communicating and relating to each other that is empty of love and even destructive.

As a teenager, I participated in the yearly summer church youth camps. One year, there was a young rap group who did part of the music for the camp that week. One of my friends hit it off with several members of the group, so I hung around with my friend and this group like a third wheel. Throughout the week, some of the group members joked around about some inappropriate things. I don't remember exactly what those things were, but I do remember one of the group member's repeated refrain, "That's coarse jokin', man." Despite his efforts to point out that the content of their humor was foul-mouthed, the rest of the group just brushed him off as if he were being too uptight. What a perfect example of the subtlety of empty words: something good and positive like humor altered just enough to pick up some out-of-place humor categories—sexual innuendo, backhanded mutterings about people we work with or for, sarcastic jabs, or something at the expense of others.

I didn't get involved in their joking, I thought. *I didn't participate,* I reasoned. No, I just listened and was silent, which might be just as bad. I was guilty by association. If they had been committing a crime, "I wasn't doing anything" wouldn't have been a valid excuse with police. Silently participating in coarse joking is actively promoting it. The same is true of all foolish talk—sarcastic jabs, gossip, slander, and the like.

Just because we aren't the ones initiating it doesn't mean that we are not participating in it. Just because we don't see the damaging effects of our words immediately doesn't mean they are not destroying our relationships. We know all this, of course, but when was the last time we let God examine our relationships? When was the last time we spent some time allowing God to scan our interactions with people at work, home, school, and church? If you are anything like me, you probably ignore the first several alerts until there is a more convenient time. That, my brothers and sisters, is a dangerous thing to do.

TOXIC ATTITUDES

Since having our first child, a son, I am amazed how much more sensitive I have become to what is being communicated and said on TV, and to what others talk about around me. I am quicker to turn the channel, and to redirect conversation with others more often. Young children are like sponges, absorbing what is going on around them. The best example of that is when kids repeat something they hear from their parents, usually in the worst possible situation and at the worst possible time. "My mommy says your house is too small," was the comment of a friend's eight-year-old daughter who was helping a family member move. The things we say and the attitudes we take toward people, church, pastors, work, friends, school, and anything or anyone else always seems to get passed on to our kids, spouses, and the people around us, even if unintentionally. The things we say and our attitudes can even influence infants. Studies show that even though babies don't understand the words that are being said, they still can detect the tone of voice and attitude. If only we were so sensitive and observant of ourselves and our attitudes.

Now, everyone has bad days that lend themselves to bad attitudes temporarily, but toxic attitudes are more long-term conditions that become ways of operating. Everyone can be discouraged and cynical at times; but if these attitudes become toxic, then they begin a perpetual state of pessimism and distrust. Everyone has things that frustrate them and even make them angry, but having toxic attitudes means we harbor those frustrations and anger until they become roots of bitterness and resentment.

BITTERNESS IS LIKE ROTTEN MILK

I take care of our son during the day. Part of taking care of him is feeding him, which is always a bottle of formula. You would think he would get sick of it, but he doesn't know anything else, so he usually guzzles it down. However, a couple of weeks ago, he fell asleep as I was feeding him and didn't finish the bottle. For whatever reason, I left the bottle in my office for the rest of the week. As you can imagine, it started to stink, get moldy, and clump up until I finally cleaned it out and took the bottle home.

When we store up bitterness and resentment against

someone, it is like keeping rotten milk around. The smell only reminds us of our hurt, reopens our wounds, and cuts us off from healing. More than that, it cuts off the possibilities of forgiveness and reconciliation, and we commit the sin of unforgiveness.

Sometimes we block the path to forgiveness by storing up bitterness and resentment against someone, but not letting them know they hurt us. We hold them responsible for the pain, but give them no chance to know about it. Unfortunately, a lot of the time, the hurt is based on a misunderstanding or a communication breakdown or simply a difference of opinion. It was something that wasn't meant to be taken the way we took it; but instead of clarifying, we hold on to it. We begin to become extremely sensitive to everything that person does and says. Everything becomes another jab at us or another smart remark. Every action is second-guessed, every motive questioned—always assuming the *worst* of that person. All along, we are only nursing bitterness and resentment, keeping it alive and well. Every new hurtful word or action (perceived or real) is like firewood added to the campfire to keep the flames burning strong. If we think it only affects that one relationship, we are kidding ourselves. It is not long before we become too sensitive in all of our relationships and new roots of bitterness are easily planted.

This is one of those subtle sins that is vigorously defended and justified when we are hurt, wronged, overlooked, stepped on, used, taken for granted, cheated, or mistreated in some way. Resentment and bitterness are much easier responses than forgiveness, and even more natural to us when someone has hurt us or wronged us. Yet, when we withhold forgiveness and build up bitterness, we enslave others and ourselves. We are not radically different than the relationships in the culture around us, and we have forgotten that we are all one in Christ. However long we hold on to that hurt, we obstruct forgiveness, and the sin of unforgiveness clings to us until we begin to ask, "What's that smell?"

CONCLUSION–KEEPING AWAKE

Maybe part of the problem is that we have been operating in these ways and others for so long that if we didn't communicate and relate in these kinds of ways, we would have trouble communicating and relating at all. We have been deceived and have deceived ourselves into thinking that it is all right to store up bitterness and resentment in our hearts, and to relate to each other in empty ways. Ultimately though, the problem is a matter of the heart. It shouldn't surprise us that the heart is where the problem begins. Jesus clearly explained that. "What comes out of a man is what makes him 'unclean.' For from within, *out of men's hearts,* come *evil thoughts,* sexual immorality, theft, murder, adultery, greed, malice, *deceit,* lewdness, envy, slander, arrogance and folly. All these evils come from *inside* and make a man 'unclean'" (Mark 7:20-23, emphasis added). "What comes out of the mouth proceeds from the heart" (Matthew 15:18, NRSV).

Our "empty words" then mean we have hearts void of or with few words of wisdom, thanksgiving, encouragement, joy, truth, love, and peace to offer to others (see Galatians 5:22-23). All we have to offer is hot air. No wonder our relationships in church are not radically different than the relationships outside church. When all we have to offer each other is hot air, relationships can only be surface-level, based on common opinions instead of God's truth, and our deepest conversations seem to be about things like weather patterns, sports, or how good our last meal was. How empty! Of course, we all long for more than that.

We all long for deeper relationships with people, especially in the church. The church is supposed to be the place where we bear one another's burdens, where we can honestly talk about our struggles, where we can talk about the major concerns of our hearts as well as the culture's biggest problems. Most of the time, though, all we can come up with is a dozen excuses why it doesn't or can't happen, or reasons to blame somebody else, so we settle for meaningless chitchat. Perhaps we really know the problem lies within our hearts.

Will you take some time now to pay attention to the alerts your heart is sending out? Instead of ignoring the alerts, will you let God show you what is found on your heart scan? Will you let God, who knows your heart and is greater than your heart, do the work that needs to be done?

When it comes to bitterness, probably the greatest first step to rid our hearts of it and resentment toward someone is prayer. Prayer *for* them. Not in the sense of explaining all the details of what they did to hurt us to God and all the reasons we are bitter or angry toward them, but prayer for God's blessings upon them. Prayer not in the sense of asking God to help them see all the ways they are wrong, but rather asking God to change our hearts, and for hearts full of love for them. Prayer not to have opportunities to show them up or to get revenge, but rather to help demonstrate the fruit of the Spirit in all our interactions with them, and that the doors of our mouths might be guarded from saying something we will regret later. Prayer in the sense of asking God for strength to not allow the bitterness and resentment back in our hearts after releasing it.

That kind of prayer takes grace. That kind of living takes grace. That kind of journeying takes a constant God-scan of our hearts and lives. Why not respond to this alert and allow God to show us and search every nook and cranny of our hearts and lives? Why not begin to take steps to make things right with others? Why not ask God to put a guard over the doors of our mouths and to guard our hearts from those things that would contaminate our words and actions? Why not seek God and ask for His grace and help? That, my brothers and sisters, is always a good thing—for our hearts to be strengthened by grace.

Scripture Cited: Psalm 19:12-13; Matthew 15:18; Mark 7:20-23; Ephesians 4:29, 31; 5:4

About the Author: Rev. Forgrave is the associate pastor of Grandview (Missouri) Church of the Nazarene.

PRIORITIES OF THE HOLY LIFE

BY JEANETTE LITTLETON

"Please, Mom! Please, please!"

No matter how much I begged, the answer was the same: the school dance would have to rock on without me. After that first year of trying to change Mom's holiness mind-set, I didn't even try anymore—and though I never would have admitted it, I didn't really care. Instead, I went to Christian banquets that were held as alternatives.

In ways, I was raised as the holiness poster child of the '60s and '70s. Besides no dances, we weren't allowed to go to movies. We were in church every time the doors were open, prayer meetings and missionary meetings included. We didn't wear makeup, but we did wear short sleeves and freely cut our hair; those old holiness rules were relaxed by the time I came along.

In the three decades since my teens, the holiness rules that were based on culture have been relaxed a lot more. While I don't have any problem with that, I also don't have any problems with the way I was raised. In fact, following the "rules" taught me great lessons on priorities of holy living.

If we're seeking to live a holy life, how will that translate in the everyday priorities of our lives? Let's consider some of the ways pursuing God makes a difference in our time, talent, and treasures.

TIME

When I married my husband, not only did he already have two young girls, 12 and 7 years old, but he also had cable TV. Before long, I discovered that unknown to her father, my oldest stepdaughter was watching television programs that weren't appropriate.

So, of course, being a family committed to Christ, we talked to our daughter and found ways to guard her from temptation.

The next thing I knew, though, *I* was the one spending hours watching cable. I wasn't watching inappropriate shows—*Green Acres* was about as racy as I got. Still, I was spending hours huddled in front of the TV. I had difficulties finding time to read my Bible, bond with my new stepchildren, and get everything accomplished that I needed to. Yet, I spent hours on the *Dick Van Dyke Show*, news reports, and *Turner Classic Movies*.

Cable was as much a temptation for me as it was for my teen stepdaughter. For me, it was a temptation to be unwise with my time.

Not too long after that, we moved away and didn't renew cable. That was one of the wisest decisions we've made. The funny thing is that once it was removed, none of us missed it very much. I didn't miss cable any more than I missed all those movies I never saw during my childhood. Instead, with that temptation removed from our lives, we learned to fill our time with other things, like relationships.

And now 10 years later, we may watch videos or DVD movies; but other than that, our television is seldom on. And a benefit is that I don't have to spend as much of my time keeping an eye on the television to make sure my kids aren't seeing things that glamorize sin, teach inappropriate values, or contradict the things we're trying to teach them about God and the Bible.

I don't believe television or cable is wrong for every believer. Nor do I believe we should never enjoy entertainment. However, I do believe as part of redeeming our time, and committing our time to the Lord, we need to evaluate the time-eaters in our lives. Perhaps the key is to evaluate how much time we're spending on whatever medium, and to discern the results of that in our lives. For instance, maybe nothing is wrong with playing games online; but if it leads us to be foolish with the resources God has given us, or leads us to enter places where we might compromise our commitment to Christ, it's often best to just avoid temptation.

Redeeming our time also means to find ways to "be Christ." For some people, that means making sure they take time to be involved in some sort of ministry. For others, it means simply remembering to exemplify Christ in interests and activities. For instance, one friend of mine serves the community by volunteering as a lead usher for the city's symphony. Not only is it a fun activity for her, but she also relishes being a witness and getting to know the other ushers, most of whom do not know Christ.

Another element to consider when we look at how we use our time is the example we set for our children. My husband pastored one church where the church secretary—who was also the children's ministry director—frequently skipped Sunday morning services to take her sons to soccer games and other sports events. What kind of priority will her children give to gathering with other believers as they grow older? Since we Wesleyans believe that God works in us and through us not just as individuals, part of our time commitment includes seeking God in a group context.

When we sanctify our time for the Lord's use, it not only means spending time to develop our relationship with Him—alone and corporately—but it also means being wise stewards of our time.

TALENT

Have you ever hated to leave work, not because you're a closet workaholic or under a deadline, but just because you have enjoyed what you're doing so much?

One day as I was working on a project, I was suddenly filled with such a sense of glory and praise—and even something that felt akin to (could it be?) worship. I was ready to grab a tissue from the box by my computer screen and wave it over the cubicle wall, just as Sister Ward waved a hankie in the air when she felt blessed during a worship service at church! As I hit the keys on my computer, I almost felt like I was wholeheartedly singing the "Hallelujah Chorus" or a stirring hymn. I felt such a sense of accomplishment and fulfillment. It was the first time that I realized that doing my work well is a way to worship God.

When we hear the word "talents," most of us probably think of people who are gifted in singing or artistry or can lead a music service or can preach an inspiring message. However, God has gifted all of us. If we can type quickly or accurately or sell an item at a store with a smile and kind word for the customer or pack items well into a box at a warehouse, these talents can be just as important as singing on stage during a church service. When we commit our abilities to Christ, we will seek ways to use our talents to further God's kingdom.

For years, I heard people talking about going on short-term mission trips, but I never signed up. Most opportunities revolved around working with street evangelism or construction—areas that are not my forté. Since I'm a klutzy introvert, these kind of situations would be more dread than worship for me. Then I talked with some people from a missions organization who had plenty of volunteers for construction and evangelism. What they really needed was some help with creating brochures and a magazine. Since I edit for a living, my ears perked up. This was the short-term mission

I'd longed for! I enjoyed two weeks with that organization, and learned that the opportunities to serve within our abilities are out there, if only we look for them.

No matter what our abilities are, we can also use them close to home to further God's kingdom. And we can do so intentionally.

Years ago in Sunday School, each week I faithfully picked up a copy of the take-home paper. I read and reread every word of every issue, and kept a complete collection for years. One of the columns I loved was called "The Back Page," written by a person named Dean Nelson,* who wrote in the character of a teen boy. In one of his simple, one-page fiction columns, he talked about tithing our time. Over the years, that concept has stayed with me.

One day I thought, *If we not only tithe our money and our time to God, shouldn't we tithe our talent too?* I began to consciously look for ways to tithe my special abilities. For me, that means sometimes taking on a job that I'd normally get paid for and doing it for free, as a tithe project, as a specific way to use my abilities for God's glory. At other times, it means consciously committing my abilities to help others, maybe even above and beyond what I'd normally do, as a special offering to God.

Setting my abilities apart to grow in holiness means determining what my abilities and spiritual gifts are, recognizing that they are God-given, and making it a priority to worship God and serve others with them.

RESOURCES

My friends Rick and Rhonda purposefully live a step beneath their abilities. They don't live in quite as nice a house as they could. They don't pour much money into their cars or home furnishings. They catch bargains and don't worry about being up-to-date.

Part of the reason they do this is that they're committed

to Christ and to seeing His kingdom grow. By living a level beneath their income, they have extra money to give to the Lord's work. I don't think they know about Wesley's mantra, which was basically, "Earn all you can, save all you can, and give all you can." But they follow it.

When I was a teenager, I first heard Nazarene evangelist Chuck Millhuff speak at a parachurch youth rally. Three decades later, I still remember how eye-opening it was for me to consider that perhaps, as Millhuff pronounced, "We can't out-give God because He has a bigger shovel." So, for some Christians, consecrating their resources includes a priority of generously giving of the finances God has given them.

There are also other ways we can use the resources God has given us for His glory. I met Aletha and Daniel shortly after my mother died. I was immediately impressed with the way they ministered to other people. They quickly took me into their home and hearts, remembering me on holidays when I had no one to celebrate with. I wasn't the only person. Their table was frequently filled with other people like me.

They also used the home God had given them for such purposes as caregiving, taking in a woman going through a tough time, for neighborhood Bible studies, and for other ministry. Even their coffeepot seemed consecrated to God, as they kept it brewing for whoever might walk in. They used their resources of home and finances to minister to others, and their time and gifts of hospitality to reach out to lonely Christians and unsaved neighbors alike.

Holiness is not just a doctrine we believe. When we're truly seeking God, it makes a difference in all areas of our lives.

Notes:
  *Dr. Nelson wrote chapter 13 of this book.

About the Author: Jeanette Littleton is a freelance writer, who lives in Gladstone, Missouri with her husband, Mark, and their children.

AN EXPANDING
VISION OF
HOLINESS

BY STAN INGERSOL

The Holiness denomination in which I was raised was probably not much different from your own. It had a fairly clear-cut identity in the 1940s and '50s. Revivals and missions were its trademarks. A strict moral code separated "us" from "the world." We were not like the big mainline denominations that we deemed guilty of theological compromise and a perverted "social gospel." Happily we left their fate to God, confident in our own destination. We were heaven-bound.

Then a funny thing happened on our way to the New Jerusalem. Somewhere along the road, the Holy Spirit convicted *us* of *our* racism. Our lily-white districts and white flight to the suburbs suddenly made us look like "less than conquerors." The Holy Spirit convicted us further of neglecting the cry of the needy at our doorstep and around the world.

And in time, we took heed and began responding. We rediscovered the city as a place of physical and spiritual need and began redirecting some of our resources there. We planted inner-city churches that combined evangelism and social compassion. We began taking world hunger seriously, set up child-sponsorship programs, and gave money for disaster relief.

The rebirth of social responsibility among Wesleyan-Holiness churches was part of a much broader Evangelical renaissance. And for once, we were not the tail-gaters at this party. Thinkers with deep roots in the Wesleyan-Holiness tradition were among those who helped to renew the Evangelical conscience, including Timothy Smith (Nazarene), Donald Dayton (Wesleyan), Howard Snyder (Free Methodist), and Ron Sider (Brethren in Christ).

Two strategies were employed as Wesleyan-Holiness churches began rethinking their mission in the contemporary world. One was to approach the Bible with new ears, and to listen more carefully to the thread of social compassion in God's name that runs from the Pentateuch through the Prophets and into the Gospels, Acts, and the Epistles.

The other strategy was to examine how Christians of other days and places have been influenced by this scriptural theme of social compassion. Does our Wesleyan-Holiness history offer concrete examples of faithful response that can serve as models or inspiration for our own faith-walk? A renewed interest in John Wesley and the Wesleyan theological tradition was linked directly with the more immediate and vital question: How should we act today? Does our history as Wesleyan-Holiness people hinder or enable a faithful response to the needy?

JOHN WESLEY AND EARLY METHODISM

The first Methodist society was composed of Oxford University students who gathered in the 1720s under the leadership of John and Charles Wesley. Their original purpose was to support one another by meeting regularly for mutual prayer, Bible study, and moral discipline, and to hold one another accountable for their academic studies.

Soon, however, these earnest young students began reaching beyond their own world of privilege and linked their pursuit of Christian holiness with ministry to the poor. They began visiting those in the debtor's prisons. In time, they also met with condemned prisoners on death row, prayed with them, and—when asked—accompanied the condemned to the gallows. Soon they were providing for other needs of the poor—food, clothing, or whatever other needs they could supply.

Methodism's subsequent development into a popular and worldwide religious movement emerged as a direct consequence of John Wesley's determination in the late 1730s to take the gospel to the poor. Several months after his famous "heartwarming experience" at Aldersgate, Wesley followed the lead of an associate, George Whitefield, and began preaching to those who labored under harsh conditions in the coal mines near England's western seaport of Bristol.

Wesley took a series of unusual steps in order to reach the poor, including outdoor preaching in the fields and streets, and the use of lay (unordained) preachers. Many of the innovations that became Methodist characteristics originated in the desire of the movement's leaders to reach the most neglected and marginalized members of society. London's slums, Bristol's docks, and impoverished mining communities like Kingswood became John Wesley's second and third homes. Wherever the poor gathered, so did the Methodists.

The history of Methodism likely would have amounted to little more than a minor paragraph in the larger history of Christian piety had Wesley not linked his "heartwarming experience" with a ministry to the poor. But Wesley took as his own the mission statement of his Master: "The Spirit of the Lord *is* upon me, because he hath anointed me to preach the gospel to the poor" (Luke 4:18, KJV).

By the 1740s, Methodism had become a glowing revival flame spreading through the British Isles. The Methodist faithful gathered in small discipleship groups to nourish their spiritual lives. They preached and testified to their faith. At the same time, they started new schools; tended to the sick; cared for orphans; and distributed medicine, food, and clothes. The growing Methodist network became an agent of spiritual, moral, and physical healing.

Concern for the downtrodden remained part of Wesley's

outlook to the very end of his life. His last letter, written on his deathbed, urged William Wilberforce, a promising young politician, to take up the cause of abolishing slavery in the British Empire. Wilberforce accepted the challenge and devoted the rest of his life to that struggle. He became the leading abolitionist of his day and always enjoyed the unwavering support of British Methodists in this great cause.

THE WESLEYAN-HOLINESS CHURCHES

American Methodism's relationship to slavery was not as exemplary as its British counterpart's however. Following Wesley's sentiments, the Methodist Episcopal Church stated its opposition to slavery at the time that it organized in Baltimore, Maryland in 1784. Almost immediately, however, it backed away from that commitment under the influence of slave-holding Methodists in the South and the imminent threat of schism. By 1840, the M. E. Church was officially mute on the divisive issue of slavery. One of today's Wesleyan-Holiness denominations came into existence precisely in reaction to that situation.

The Wesleyan Methodist Connection emerged in 1843 under the leadership of an abolitionist minister named Orange Scott. Scott originally was a minister in the M. E. Church's New England Conference, where he sought to awaken the consciences of fellow Methodists against slavery. At one point, he purchased subscriptions to an abolitionist paper for each minister in the conference. Eventually he launched his own paper, *The True Wesleyan*, to advocate his view that "true Wesleyans" should work for the liberation of the slaves.

He and like-minded Methodists concluded after the General Conference of 1840 that antislavery reform was impossible within the main branch of Methodism. They decided to break away, form their own connection of churches, and labor unhindered in the abolition cause. Thus, the oldest

Wesleyan-Holiness denomination in America was born out of commitment to a great social cause.

The rich heritage of the Wesleys and early Methodism is shared in other ways by Wesleyan-Holiness churches. One of these —The Salvation Army—has shaped its inner life around a mission to the poor more fully than any other church in history.

The Salvation Army began in London's slums, founded by William and Catherine Booth. Its original name was the Christian Mission, and it functioned initially as an evangelistic agency. However, William Booth's perspective gradually changed as he evangelized among the poor. The Booths began to incorporate social work into their ministry. Eventually they reorganized the ministry under the name Salvation Army, concluding that military-type discipline was vital to sustain the work of religious and social reform among the urban poor. In 1890, William Booth published his analysis of England's social problems, *In Darkest England, and the Way Out*—a book advocating broad social reform.

The Salvation Army came to be characterized by evangelistic street meetings and soup kitchens, vibrant worship in rented halls and the distribution of food and clothing, strong holiness preaching and literacy programs, and dozens of other expressions of compassion in Christ's name. Over the years, it has remained true to the vision of its founders; and like early Methodism, it aims at spiritual, moral, and physical healing. It can be found today on every inhabited continent, working to shelter the homeless or to mitigate gang violence. The urban poor remain the primary focus of its ministry.

Phoebe Palmer was the remarkable Methodist laywoman sometimes referred to as the "Mother of the American Holiness Movement." She, too, exemplified the union of vital piety and social concern. Palmer is remembered primarily for her preaching, writing, and general leadership of the first phase of the 19th-century holiness revival. Palmer was also one of the leaders in a project sponsored by Methodist

women that established the Five Points Mission in New
York City's slums. The Five Points Mission rescued young
girls from lives of prostitution, operated a day school for
poor children, arranged adoptions, fought the saloon trade,
and conducted worship. A large five-story building was
erected in 1853 to house these ministries and more, including the distribution of clothing and a library used by working men in the evenings.

Others imitated the Five Points Mission in the Wesleyan-Holiness Movement. Theodore and Manie Ferguson,
for instance, founded the Peniel Mission in the Los Angeles
slums in 1894. Like the Five Points Mission, the Peniel
Mission was housed in a substantial building and provided a
wide range of relief to the homeless and the poor. Peniel
Missions eventually were established in most major cities of
the West Coast.

The antislavery impulse that spawned the Wesleyan
Methodist Connection was also a motivation of Benjamin
Titus Roberts, founder of the Free Methodist Church. However, Roberts also dissented from the Methodist Episcopal
Church for another reason. He strongly objected to pew
rentals—a method that city churches increasingly used to
raise money. Pew rentals discriminated against the poor. The
well-to-do reserved the best seats in the sanctuary. Those
who could not afford to rent pews sat in less desirable seats.
The very practice cried "unwelcome!" to the poor.

Roberts urged his congregation in Rochester, New York
to change its practice. His laypeople refused. Roberts then
urged the Methodist churches across the city to cooperate in
planting one or more "free" churches. Even that did not happen, so Roberts broke with the Methodist church in 1860
and established the type of congregation he felt called of God
to form. From the outset, the name "Free Methodist" was intended to convey two ideas: free persons (antislavery) and free
pews (the poor were welcome in churches of this name).

Phineas Bresee was another who accepted the challenge

of ministering to the needs of the urban poor. By 1894, Bresee had served every large Methodist church around Los Angeles as the area district superintendent. In that year, he asked to be appointed to inner-city mission work. The request was refused, so Bresee stepped aside from the Methodist ministry.

For a year, he served as the Sunday morning preacher at the Peniel Mission. Then he joined others to launch a new church in downtown Los Angeles. J. P. Widney, a physician, suggested the name "Church of the Nazarene," pointing out that it identified the congregation with "the toiling, lowly mission of Christ."[1]

The congregation met in rented halls for several months before constructing a simple board church that was soon dubbed "the Glory Barn." Bresee said, "We want places so plain that every board says welcome to the poorest." He continued: "Let the Church of the Nazarene be true to its commission; not great and elegant buildings; but to feed the hungry and clothe the naked, and wipe away the tears of sorrowing; and gather jewels for His diadem."[2]

Seth C. Rees, an evangelical Quaker, was another holiness revivalist who ministered to social outcasts and inspired others to do so. Urban poverty turned some young girls toward prostitution, so Rees inspired a small network of homes for unwed mothers known as Rest Cottages. The network was small, but spanned the United States. Wesleyan Methodists, Nazarenes, and others sponsored various homes in this chain. A similar ministry was organized in Texas by J. T. Upchurch, whose Berachah Rescue Society reached out to errant girls in the slums of Dallas, Fort Worth, and Waco.

Other Wesleyan-Holiness denominations have shown their commitment to the welfare of others through their concerted efforts at peacemaking. The Evangelical Friends and the Brethren in Christ both have roots in the Christian pacifist tradition. Both denominations incorporated the primary emphasis of the Wesleyan-Holiness revival into their identities in the late 19th century. In the 20th century, these denominations, with other pacifist groups, have interpreted their role as "peace churches" much more broadly than in earlier days. At one time, they saw their role as "peace churches" in terms of refraining from war. Today, they see peacemaking as something active, rather than reactive. They teach conflict resolution and sponsor ministries that reconcile people and groups to one another. Norval Hadley, an Evangelical Friend, played a key role in the New Call to Peacemaking that re-energized the peace churches in the 1970s. During the same period, Ron Sider of the Brethren in Christ focused the eyes of many Christians to the problem of world hunger in his best-selling book, *Rich Christians in an Age of Hunger.*

A KINGDOM PEOPLE

There are several reasons why Christians should care for the bodies, as well as the spirits, of others. However, the primary reason is that we should be, as Paul urged us, imitators of Christ.

Luke records the beginning of Jesus' ministry in 4:14-21. At the synagogue in Nazareth, Jesus was handed the Isaiah scroll. He read a portion that indicated God's love for those who are forsaken. "The Spirit of the Lord is on me, because he has anointed me to preach good news to the poor. He has sent me to proclaim freedom for the prisoners and recovery of sight for the blind, to release the oppressed, to proclaim the year of the Lord's favor" (vv. 18-19). It was no accident that, near the outset of His ministry, He read and commented upon these particular verses. They summed up the heart of His ministry to people.

In Luke 7:11-23, we see Jesus going about His remarkable ministry and John the Baptist's disciples coming to check Him out. Jesus' response to them shows that His ministry was properly focused on the most needy in society. "Re-

port to John what you have seen and heard: The blind receive sight, the lame walk, those who have leprosy are cured,
the deaf hear, the dead are raised, and the good news is
preached to the poor" (v. 22).

The healing stories in the ministry of Jesus provide great
insight into the character of God and the nature of God's
kingdom. The dominant theme of Jesus' preaching was that
the kingdom of God was at hand through Jesus' own presence and ministry. The compassionate works of Jesus toward
the blind, the lame, and even the dead were not intended to
be merely vivid demonstrations of power. There were, after
all, other "miracle workers" in that day. Rather, these were un-
mistakable, obvious signs of God's kingdom breaking into
history. Jesus' answer to the disciples of John the Baptist
pointed toward the righteousness of His acts of mercy, not
just to the power with which He accomplished them. The
kingdom of God has its very basis in God's great love!

When Jesus returned to the One whom He called His
"Father in heaven" (see Matthew 12:50), He left behind His
church to carry on His ministry of reconciliation. It is now
our mission to announce how God's kingdom breaks into human affairs. When Christians feed the hungry, care for the
sick, provide for orphans and widows, or educate the illiterate
in Christ's name, we are showing the world that the kingdom
of God is at hand—that it is here, among us, right now.

We are already participating, in all likelihood, in some
form of social ministry—at least indirectly. When we give
tithes and offerings to our local churches, for instance, a portion of that goes to support missionaries who provide medical assistance and teach basic literacy in parts of the world
where these are sorely needed. Some of our tithe may also
support church-based orphanages, inner-city rescue missions, soup kitchens, or facilities for unwed mothers in far-
flung places.

Still, the call to discipleship urges us to something deeper than only indirect ministry. We are called as Christians to

be God's ministers in the world. Our pastors are called to equip us for ministry, but we—the people of God—are God's hands and feet at this particular point in human history.

Look around at your own congregation. Is it a place where the hungry or the homeless would turn in their need? If so, then why? If not, then why not? Would your congregation's testimony to the wider community be more credible or less credible if it was involved more deeply in some form of social ministry?

Some Wesleyan-Holiness congregations have started new social ministries over the past two decades when "mission groups" have formed within congregations. In some cases, mission groups have started ministries to those dying of AIDS. Other mission groups have worked in soup kitchens, participated with Christians of other denominations in building low-cost homes, or served as conflict mediators.

The redemptive work of God through Christ frees us from sin and sets us free to serve others. The ways in which we can do so are as unbounded as the sea of human need.

Notes:

1. Timothy L. Smith, *Called Unto Holiness* (Kansas City: Nazarene Publishing House, 1962), 111.

2. Phineas Bresee, Editorial, *The Nazarene Messenger,* January 15, 1902, 6.

Scripture Cited: Luke 4:14-21; 7:11-23

About the Author: Dr. Ingersol serves as the archivist for the Church of the Nazarene at its International Center in Kansas City, Missouri.

HOLINESS AND CULTURE

BY JON JOHNSTON

There seems to be no escape from the endless string of intrusive commercials:

- Airplanes tow banners over beaches to advertise amusement parks
- Clouds are rearranged to spell the name of a cola
- Stadiums are named for corporations
- Television news is advertised on tiny screens at gasoline pumps.

The Super Bowl stages two major competitions: a football game and a contest to determine the winning commercial. The way we're headed, I envision some future war being sponsored by a chocolate maker, or maybe a church renamed for a telecommunications company—to eliminate the need for having a building fund.

However, we need not wear a corporation's uniform (like race car drivers), launch a big company balloon, or purchase a 30-second sound bite to send a product message. In a real sense, we constantly advertise our "goods" by whatever we project to those around us. This is especially true for us who claim to be twice-born.

A MULTIPURPOSE PRODUCT WITH LONGEVITY

What must our bold message be to today's culture? The same one proclaimed by Paul two millennia ago: "Do not conform any longer to the pattern of this world, but be *transformed* by the renewing of your mind" (Romans 12:2, emphasis added). The world offers skewed, distorted values based on privilege, power, and possessions. Making these our highest priorities invariably leads to our demise.

Our blessed Lord offers the grand alternative: transformation. When pondering this word, I cannot help thinking of two things: a butterfly and a sailboat. The first suggests a glorious metamorphosis; whereas, a sailboat carries ballast weight to prevent it from capsizing. Transformation provides us with a new nature—we become truly holy through and through. But in addition, we gain spiritual ballast for life's inevitable storms.

Transformation sells itself, *if* proclaimed by those who are living incarnations of its reality. It is positive, pragmatic, and powerful. Something to aspire for and rejoice in. Even the secular world uses the powerful concept to its advantage. We hear of transformed perspectives, bodies, earning potential. But no transformation compares to the miracle of a transformed heart, which is precisely what our Lord generously offers.

STICKER SHOCK

So, why is a truth so obvious to us vehemently resisted by our culture? It's the identical reason people shy away from buying an expensive new car—"sticker shock." An incredibly steep price. The same impediment that dissuades people from undergoing the rigorous training demanded of all long-distance endurance runners.

Regrettably, secular culture overlooks one crucial fact: the high cost for transformation has already been paid by our Lord (see Titus 3:4-7). We need only acknowledge our need for His gift, receive it by faith, and utilize it to "advertise" His unfathomable love to others.

Still, this offer we "just can't refuse" is refused. Scores

chart their own misguided course to their own detriment (see Proverbs 14:12). Some congratulate themselves for attaining a measure of good works and achieving high ethical standards, unaware that their self-generated efforts only push them farther away from God-dependency.

Others, similar to insurgents in wars, boldly attack believers. They erect roadblocks and clever traps, and toss many "verbal grenades." We're accused of being judgmental and intolerant for merely sharing our beliefs. Like in Roman times, we're called "divisive," when our sole intent is to see everyone unified in Christ.

We're said to constitute a threat to free speech, to the existence of other religions, to civility, and even to the Constitution! And like snowballs, some of these bogus accusations stick in the minds of people who have no occasion to learn the real truth.

How must we respond? As always, it behooves us to focus on cues and clues derived from the teachings and example of our Lord. How does He advise approaching a secular culture that increasingly resists His generous grace, and along with it, rejects His faithful servants?

A CAFETERIA OF CHOICES

In his classic work, *Christ and Culture,* H. Richard Niebuhr presents five options for relating Christ and culture. Let's briefly consider each.

1. *Christ Against Culture.* Jesus vehemently opposes sin-ravaged, polluted culture in all of its debauched forms. So should we.
2. *Christ of Culture.* Christ and culture are in fundamental agreement (e.g., democracy inculcates His teachings and motherly love reflects His nature).
3. *Christ Above Culture.* Our Lord transcends culture and offers it light and guidance (see Luke 1:79).
4. *Christ and Culture in Paradox.* Jesus recognizes that

both have authority, though they are neither congru-
ent nor equal in value (see Matthew 22:21).

5. *Christ the Transformer of Culture.* Christ accepts spiritually bankrupt culture and radically changes it. The
   disfigured become transfigured![1]

All five contain elements of truth, based on time and
circumstance. Nevertheless, the final one comes closest to
defining our missional task. Jesus yearns to renovate, restore,
and reclaim our sin-sick culture by transforming its inhabi-
tants one at a time, through and through. And He does so by
renewing, or transforming, minds (see Romans 12:2).

ON THE OFFENSIVE WITH FAITH

Allow me to suggest four good reasons why we continue
running our race with optimism and constantly reinvigorated
spirits—in spite of opposition. Why we cannot resist taking
the offensive in witnessing to Christ's transforming power.
Why we're spurred onward in faith.

*First, in spite of immorality in high places, we see reasons
for hope.* When we consider the term "hope" today, our
minds think of something improbable but remotely possible.
In God's Word, the meaning is much more definitive and
definite. Biblical hope is based on the faith that something is
guaranteed to occur (e.g., the hope of our salvation).

In that biblical context, multitudes pray for world leaders. The kingdom of God continues to grow, even in the face
of unprecedented, constant, and intense persecution. Christians are marshaling forces to make a difference for the spiritually and materially impoverished, destitute, and deprived.
Revival fires burn on our planet!

Second, the tide may be turning in the cultural war.
Richard Nadler notes in *National Review* that most social
pathologies seem to actually be declining. Divorce rates are
down 19 percent since 1981. The birth rate for unmarried
teens is down 7.5 percent since 1994. And the latter is not

accounted for by increased abortion, for it, too, is down 15.3 percent since 1990. Evidently, the spiral upward has been curtailed—at least for a while.

What's more, morality appears to be an increasing concern. Respondents to a recent survey ranked it "No. 1" in importance in the selection of any national leader. Granted, there's still an oversupply of evil out there, but we could be starting to turn the corner. As the salt, light, and leaven of this world, we're starting to make a difference!

Third, the strong challenges we've recently faced seem to have toughened us up. Some of us recall the '70s, when evangelical Christianity was showcased and praised.[2] Born-againers were lavished with popularity. Unfortunately, all of those "strokes" created an atmosphere of complacency. Televangelist scandals flourished and church attendance plummeted. We became "soft" in our underbellies.

Today, Christians—and most everything they stand for—are targeted continuously by atheistic groups and politically sensitive corporations (e.g., agreeing to not having customers wished a "Merry Christmas"). It's so intense that many conclude that Christianity has little significant influence on the culture. This negativity is uncovered by recent books like *Slouching Towards Gomorrah* (Robert Bork), *Against the Night: Living in the New Dark Ages* (Charles Colson), and *Blinded by Might* (Cal Thomas).

Nevertheless, from these Christian-bashing times—when those of us who are devoted to our faith are derogatorily tagged "radical right-wing conservatives"—has emerged an increasingly courageous, outspoken, and effective remnant. Indeed, our influence is being felt within government, education, bioethics, and around office water coolers. Believers are speaking out, answering back, standing tall. And it's spiritually refreshing to witness!

Finally, a new worldview called "postmodernism" has invaded society. Without question, many of its positions challenge biblical teachings. To state a few:

- There is no such thing as Truth
- Emotion is a better guide than reason
- Only power is worth striving for, since everyone strives for it alone
- The individual is merely a "mouthpiece" for culture.

The threat of this philosophy has toughened us up even more. As "good soldier[s] of Christ Jesus" (2 Timothy 2:3), many of us clearly see the big battle looming, and we are intently preparing for the fight. Apologetics, or the defense of the faith, is a rapidly expanding field of study in Christian higher education.

Nevertheless, on a more uplifting note, postmodernism has done something else: it has provided us Christians with a legitimate place at the table of dialogue. For many years, its predecessor, modernism or scientism—with its blatant rejection of the supernatural, completely rejected our message. Now, at least, we're given an invitation to speak our piece, even though, admittedly, we're considered just one voice among many.

Quoting the late president of Nazarene Theological Seminary, Lewis T. Corlett, considering these positive changes, it's time to "bless God and take courage." Perhaps what we're advertising is starting to penetrate. Our ideas are beginning to germinate. With this in mind, it behooves us to keep replaying our glorious message to a culture that so desperately needs our blessed Lord's authentic, life-giving, sanctifying transformation.

Still, we must ask, what impact does God's gift of transformation have on our personal lives? Does it make us starchy, self-righteous, elevated above others' trials? Do we become filled with wisdom and perpetual happiness?

WHAT IS OUR "ADDED VALUE"?

In spite of what naysayers may charge, Eugene H. Peterson explains that authentic Christians are definitely *not:*

- *fussy* moralists who cluck their tongues over a world going to hell; they *are* people who praise the God who is on their side;
- *pious pretenders* in the midst of a decadent culture; they *are* robust witnesses to the God who is our help; nor,
- *fatigued outcasts* who carry righteousness as a burden in a world where the wicked flourish; they *are* people who sing "Oh, blessed be God!" . . . who does not abandon us defenseless![3]

For starters, though transformed in heart and life, we share many aspects of the human condition with our nonbelieving counterparts. For example, we have the same need for protection and security. Nevertheless, our distinctive is that we have no need to erect our own defenses. As the psalmist declares: "God is our refuge and strength, an ever-present help in trouble. Therefore we will not fear" (Psalm 46:1).

When it pertains to our personal well-being, we need not lapse into paranoia—constantly glancing over our shoulders lest evil overtake us, nor gaze on our footsteps lest we inadvertently slip. God is on our side. He is "behind and before" us (Psalm 139:5). In short, we have the confidence that we're covered! And that provides jubilation in our hearts. Again, Peterson finds just the right words to describe it:

We speak our words of praise in a world that is hellish; we sing our songs of victory in a world where things get messy; we live our joy among people who neither understand nor encourage us.

But the content of our lives is God, not humanity. We are not scavenging in the dark alleys of the world, poking in its garbage cans for a bare subsistence. We are traveling in the light, toward God who is rich in mercy and strong to save. *It is Christ, not culture, that defines our lives. It is the help we experience, not the hazards we risk that shapes our lives*[4] (emphasis added).

Once again, our Lord's gift of transformation is the key.

WELCOME TO THE FISH TANK!

We must never gloss over the fact that this world is an unfriendly environment for those of us who faithfully walk the Christian pathway. Simply stated, we're at cross-purposes, which has prompted extreme tribulation for God's people. Jesus was adamant: If we love Him, we'll be hated by the world (see Luke 21:17). The old chorus hit the bull's eye: "This world is not [our] home, we're just a-travlin' through."[5]

For that reason, we've been called names that imply our loose connection with this planet and its intrusive influences—names like "sojourner," "pilgrim," "traveler," "alien." The Bible strongly advises us to keep our primary gaze heavenward, and to not "sink our roots" deeply in the soil of this earth. Our treasure is located in a glorious place where rust and moth do not corrupt (see Matthew 6:19-20). It is a place of lasting joy, surrounded by the saints and angels, and with our precious Lord.

Meanwhile, here we're stuck for a significant spate of time. Again, we'll be repeatedly reminded that our environment is harsh, and at times, even brutal. Any vast reclamation project we might have in mind to turn it into a moral place is doomed to fail. Creating heaven on earth is far beyond the realm of our capability, no matter how ingenious or sincere we might be.

What is the answer? Put simply, we must allow the Savior to create His environment within us—and to transport and transmit it wherever we go. When such transformation takes place, we need not fear being adversely impacted by the cultural corruption that engulfs us.

This reality causes my mind to picture what I witnessed transpiring at an aquatic park. A fish tank contained briny, polluted seawater straight from the Pacific Ocean. Inside it were all species of marine life imaginable. Suddenly, a skilled diver joined his "friends" in their environment. And he did so without trepidation or concern for his well-being.

Was he in an alien environment? You bet. A gulp or inhalation of water would have "punched his ticket" in short order. His realization of this fact prompted him to wear an airtight helmet, containing life-sustaining oxygen, channeled to him through a tube that went to a surface pump. He survived and thrived, in effect, because he brought along his own environment—one that was conducive to maintaining life.

In a real sense, we're very similar to divers immersed in a "cultural tank" that is saturated with pollution to the brim. Ingesting even a small amount of what surrounds us means inviting spiritual death.

However, our blessed Lord invites us to be transformed with His life-giving Presence, permitting us to go anywhere without fear or insecurity. Why? Because His transformation is like oxygen for the diver. But it not only sustains life, it enhances it to the fullest! In His triumphant words: "I am come that they might have life, and that they might have it more abundantly" (John 10:10, KJV).

With this image in our minds, let's join together with a ringing, unceasing song of victory on our lips, and a joyful anticipation in our hearts. It is *that* very song that will be our best, and most convincing, advertisement in this sin-weary world!

Notes:

1. H. Richard Niebuhr, *Christ and Culture* (Scranton, Pa.: Harper Collins, 1956).

2. Eugene H. Peterson, *A Long Obedience in the Same Direction* (Colorado Springs: Inter-Varsity Press, 2000), 77.

3. Peterson, 85-86.

4. Peterson, 79.

5. Chorus entitled "Do Lord." Author unknown.

Scripture Cited: Psalms 46:1; 139:5; John 10:10; Romans 12:2; 2 Timothy 2:3

About the Author: Dr. Johnston teaches sociology at Pepperdine University in Malibu, California.

LIVING IN THE REAL WORLD

BY DEAN NELSON

Part of my daughter's ritual when she came home each day from middle school was to empty the contents of her backpack on the kitchen table. Some of the first items extracted were announcements on brightly colored paper:

- Students will read their poetry at the "Koffee Haus" next Thursday. Espresso machine provided by Beanz, the local coffee shop. Please express your appreciation to the manager.
- Yearbook pictures will be taken next week. No spaghetti straps or low-cut tops allowed.
- Band practice will resume on Tuesdays at 7:30 A.M.
- Human sexuality will be taught in science classes next month. If you want your student excused from this teaching segment, sign the enclosed waiver and send it in to the office.

My wife and I usually read the announcements, noted them in our calendars, and tossed them in the recycling basket. Total time at home for these messages: maybe 10 minutes.

Except for one.

It announced a program called "Dads at Lunch." I was intrigued by its simplicity, and moved, maybe a little, by guilt. The school was asking dads to come to the school during the lunch period and just hang out with the kids. Not be a cop, not be a buddy, not help with homework. Just hang out.

121

It was inconvenient for sure. The only two days of the week I could do it were designated writing days. This would be an interruption right in the middle of my most creative surges. I knew that, even if I got on a roll and everything in my right brain was clicking, I'd constantly be checking that little clock in the corner of my screen to see how much time I had before I needed to head to the school. Hemingway reportedly said that if he knew he had an appointment later in the afternoon, he simply couldn't write that day. I'm there with you, Poppa.

But still.

Here was a chance to be a participant in my community, without having to be an assistant coach every weekend or buy something at the neighborhood craft fair.

The flyer got moved from surface to surface in the house for about two weeks. I approached my seventh-grade daughter.

"What do you think of my doing this?" I asked, holding the announcement.

She barely looked up. "It's fine. Just don't embarrass me. I don't have to talk to you when you're there, do I?"

"No, I won't even look your direction. Tell me where you sit, and I'll avoid the area completely."

She drew a map of the outdoor lunch area and placed Xs on different regions. She sat with her scout troop here. The girls of ill-repute (insert your own euphemism) sat there. The athletes sat there. The druggies sat there. The rich kids sat there. The misfits scattered through there, but didn't really sit with each other. The African-Americans sat there, the Hispanics sat there, the Asians sat there. The Bible Club sat there.

As much as the world has changed since I was in junior high, this diagram depressed me. It meant that, in all of the improvements in the human race since I had been in seventh grade, the Invisible Hand was still shaking the Sifter, separating the cool from the uncool, the "in" crowd from the rejects. Despite our enlightened selves, we still tribalize and isolate and punish.

When I checked in at the front office, the receptionist gave me a button that identified me as a "DAD AT LUNCH." She also handed me a few coupons, good for a free cheeseburger at the local fast-food chain.

"These are if you catch one of the kids being good," she said. *Interesting word choice,* I thought. I noticed the drawer where the coupons are kept must have had a thousand in there. At the rate she was handing them to me, my grandchildren would be students here before the coupons were used up.

"Define 'being good,'" I said.

"If they speak to you, or if they throw away some trash," she said. "Just don't give coupons to kids with plastic bags who are picking up trash." Apparently they had been caught for doing something else.

"Do I have to have a reason to give one of these coupons out?"

She thought for a moment, and shrugged. "I guess not."

"Then can I have some more?"

I looked for students sitting alone and sat briefly with many of them, trying to engage them in conversation, trying hard not to act with condescension or pity, trying not to listen to the sound of the shaking Sifter reminding me of my own junior high lunch experiences, trying to ignore the cheapness of the large stereo speakers blaring distorted hip-hop music. I asked the students about classes and teachers and books. Some were very talkative, even effusive, revealing the reasons why people steered clear of them. One barely seemed to endure my questioning and said, finally, "I prefer to be by myself, if you don't mind."

"Really?" I said. "Why?"

"Because people annoy me. They're so stupid."

At the end of each brief conversation, I produced a coupon.

"What is this for?" they would ask. I told them it was for a free cheeseburger.

"No, what did we do to deserve it?"

"Nothing. I just wanted you to have it. No reason. Just because I want to."

Some were thankful. Most walked away quizzical. Some showed their friends, and those friends came to ask for a coupon. At this point, I felt comfortable attaching requirements.

"You see that kid sitting over there by himself? Walk over there, sit down, and tell him something good about himself," I would say before giving the coupon.

Some kids caught on to the coupon gig pretty quickly, and, when they saw me, started helping others with their backpacks, throwing trash away, looking my direction out of the corners of their eyes. One girl made sure that she was always in my line of vision, and that I saw her do something nice. She got a coupon, but it's not much fun handing out coupons to people like that. It's boring.

If I saw trouble brewing in a group (shouting, cursing, shoving, name-calling, and swinging backpacks were my indicators), I would walk into the middle of the circle with the coupons. "Look at this," I'd say. "Free cheeseburgers. Anybody want one?" They all did. Crisis averted.

A few of the tables had checkerboards painted onto their surfaces, so some days I brought checkers from home. All it took was sitting down and setting the checkers on the board, and kids would appear like snowboarders around the last can of energy drink, wanting to play. The sound around the game was deafening. My opponent was a posse: "No, don't move there, stupid! He'll jump you!" And every move a kid made was followed by a Greek Chorus of the obligatory middle-school mantra: "You suck!" Everyone got a coupon just for being in the crowd. Occasionally I would catch my daughter's eye as she watched the chaos from a distance. I got a nod and a smile.

The cacophony of the lunch period built to an ear-bleeding pitch, and then the bell rang, signaling a return to classes. The place cleared out as quickly as cockroaches when you turn on the kitchen light. Then the crows and gulls parachuted in like an airborne division, and created a chaos of their own. None were interested in playing checkers.

Long after I returned home from the lunches, I would think about them and wonder why I sensed more wholeness handing out coupons than I have experienced in practically anything else I have done in my life. Eventually I began thinking about one of the Church's ancient sacraments: Vocation. Not the vocation of middle-schoolers. Mine.

The ancient sacrament of receiving a vocational call centers on seeing a greater purpose for using our gifts, skills, and interests, instead of just practicing a trade. The vocational call is discovering that we can best use our skills, gifts, and interests for the good of others. It is one of the ways we experience God, and one of the ways we help the world experience the same. The vocational call on all of us is to continue and extend the work of grace and love in the world. Those are our "holy orders." As we accept the work we are to do, or search for the kind of work we wish to do, the sacramental approach to it is to allow the search be under the umbrella of this sacred call. The work we do and wish to do is one of the means toward discovering who we are and what our role is in the world. Our unique talents, desires, and backgrounds are the means by which we fulfill that calling. And by looking at it as a calling, we experience the sacred throughout our day. We experience the presence of God through the exercise of our abilities.

This sacramental view of calling took an increasingly exclusive turn, as did most of the sacraments, as religious practice evolved. Instead of the vocational call being on all of us, it became more of the territory of those called into certain kinds of service. As the term "holy orders" evolved, it became interpreted to mean "withdrawn" and "dedicated," usually into the cloister of a convent or monastery. It grew into a type of elitism.

But it wasn't always that way, and it doesn't have to be that way now, if we truly believe that God is breaking through into every moment, and is visible to those who are paying attention. The true call on all of us is not to withdraw, but to engage. Work and worship can be woven into the same cloth.

The poet Donald Hall said, "There are jobs, there are chores, and there is work."[1] Our jobs are how we make money so that we can pay bills. Our chores are the things we do to keep the organization—a family, for instance—from falling into chaos. That explanation falls on deaf ears with my daughter, but I still think it's true.

But our work? "As long as it is day, we must do the work of him who sent me. Night is coming, when no one can work" (John 9:4). And what is that work? To summarize Paul's letters, it is to participate in the redeeming, reconciling, restoring activity of God in the world. There is opportunity for vocation in every occupation, because the vocation of everyone is to point to the presence of God, with or without a script of a specific job.

Or, as the character says in Frederick Buechner's novel *Brendan*, "To lend each other a hand when we're falling. Perhaps that's the only work that matters in the end."[2]

Marcia, my wife, is an accountant. That's her occupation. She has an MBA from a major university, and has used her accounting and finance skills to help construction companies build buildings and make money. Her employers are not in business to build shelters for the homeless or churches for the devout; although, since her present bosses are spiritually minded, that is part of what they do. Mostly, though, they build office buildings. It is a responsible, fair company. And until recently, she felt that her vocation was to help that company stay in a strong financial position, as well as be a positive influence to those she encountered throughout the day.

Then she was introduced to an organization called Stephen Ministries. With some training, Stephen Ministers provide compassionate care to persons in personal crisis. The relationship between the Stephen Minister and the one in need can last weeks, months, or longer. The ministers don't provide money or advice. They are trained to avoid the temptation to solve problems and meet specific needs. They simply provide a compassionate presence to people who can't continue on their own. They give people the opportunity for their troubled hearts to rest. The only thing that Stephen Ministers can promise is that they will listen to those who need them, and that they will pray for them. By being a Stephen Minister, Marcia made a major discovery. Despite the fact that she had a job, she discovered her vocation. "I know what I am put on earth to do," she told me.

Holiness, as it is practiced every day, is not simply a moral code or a list of ethical principles, in my opinion. It is living out our vocation, participating in God's great work. It is handing out coupons, literally or figuratively. It is acknowledging those who get ignored by everyone else, listening and not advising. These are things everyone can do. That doesn't mean we go find the misfits and give them a trinket and a pat on the head. It means we can look for those in our families, our places of work, and in our communities who routinely are ignored, passed over, or taken advantage of; and we can, in one way or another, say to them, "I see you. I notice you. You're not invisible. You matter." It may be the only way they will know that God sees them too.

Loneliness is the most devastating disease in the world. Jesus noticed everyone, including those out on the margins. We must work the works of Him who sent Jesus.

Vocation is where the desires of our heart intersect with the needs of the world. My occupation is writer and university professor, but my vocation is something else—something I am called into throughout each day.

In the novel *Lying Awake* by Mark Salzman, the main

character, Sister John of the Cross, becomes confused in her spiritual calling at the convent where she lives. The visions she used to have no longer occur, now that her epilepsy has been successfully treated by a doctor. (An interesting sub-theme in Salzman's writings is that he links spirituality to mental illness.) At the end of the novel, her Mother Superior approaches her and asks if she will give a novice sister spiritual direction on God's will.

"I don't feel I know anything about God's will, Mother," said Sister John.

"Yet you're still here, trying to do His will anyway," Mother Emmanuel said. "That's the kind of understanding I meant. The doing kind, not the knowing kind."

Both women then watch as birds busily work and call around the fountain in the garden. The birds "seemed to have the best understanding of all," Salzman writes. "They answered yes to everything."[3]

Handing out coupons meant I was saying "yes" to the great work. A coupon as evidence of a holy order? I wonder what other sacraments might be in my daughter's backpack.

Notes:

1. Donald Hall, *Life Work* (Boston: Beacon Press, 2003), 4.

2. Frederick Buechner, *Brendan* (San Francisco: Harper, 1988), 217.

3. Mark Salzman, *Lying Awake* (New York: Random House, 2000), 181.

Scripture Cited: John 9:4

About the Author: Dr. Nelson is the director of the journalism program at Point Loma Nazarene University in San Diego. His work has appeared in the *New York Times*, the *Boston Globe*, *Christianity Today*, *Holiness Today*, and several other national publications. He has written 11 books, most recently a collaboration with Dr. Gary Morsch of Heart to Heart International, called *The Power of Serving Others*.